SCRIBBLING YARMOUTH NA'

An edited selection from the writings of
Arthur Henry Patterson, A.L.S.
(John Knowlittle)

By
Beryl Tooley

First Published in 2004 by

BERYL TOOLEY
"Trinity", The Street, North Cove
Beccles, Suffolk, NR34 7PN

Copyright © Beryl Tooley, 2004

ISBN 0-9549048-0-X

Printed in England by
BLACKWELL JOHN BUCKLE
Charles Street, Great Yarmouth, Norfolk

CONTENTS

ACKNOWLEDGEMENTS

I am grateful to the County Archivist at the Norfolk Record Office at the Archive Centre for assistance in researching the manuscripts of Arthur Henry Patterson. The main sources have been from the following:

    Notebooks: 1878-1935, Mss. 513-543, 4134-4146;

    Some autobiographical reminiscences, 1916, Ms. 4181; Personal reminiscences, 1916, vol. 1., Ms. 4209; Reminiscences of a Norfolk Naturalist, Ms. 4210; Yarmouth memories of the 60s and 70s., Ms. 4208; Another dose of reminiscences, Ms. 4166; Reminiscences of a School Attendance Officer, Ms. 4165

Other sources:

The published books of Arthur Patterson, in the author's own collection, as listed in Part 1 of the Bibliography.

The Patterson Collection, Natural History Museum, Norwich Castle (thanks to Tony Urwin for his help).

Personal diaries of Frederick Cook in the custody of Suffolk Record Office, Lowestoft Central Library.

I have also made reference to *The Beachman*, by David Higgins (Terence Dalton, 1987).

Every effort has been made to establish copyright for the images used.

I am grateful to the following for the use of black and white photographs:

    Peter Allard, page 30

    Percy Trett, page 14, 16, 55 (Fishermen's Hospital), 59

    Eastern Daily Press, page 94

    Great Yarmouth Mercury Archives, page 64

    Ivan Gould, page 133

Special thanks to
Keith Skipper for writing the foreward,
Ian Hinton for his expertise in the design and artwork,
Ian Sargen for proof-reading,
John Heasman for his support and encouragement,
and
my family for their help and patience when, at times,
undoubtedly AP appeared to take over my life.

**This book is dedicated to my husband, John, who died in 1996.
He was the inspiration for my love of the marshes,
Breydon and the Broads.**

FOREWORD

The title of this engrossing volume is perfectly in keeping with Arthur Patterson's gloriously self-effacing pen-name of John Knowlittle. These "scribblings" form an important part of our priceless natural history heritage. He was such a prolific writer it must have been quite a task for his great-grand-daughter to confine herself to a comparatively small selection from such a bounty. Even so, Beryl has chosen well to offer a telling insight into the man and his many outdoor missions, especially on and around his beloved Breydon Water.

The passion of a self-taught enthusiast shines through all these excerpts – I suggest those initials A.L.S. after his name ought to stand for Always Learning Something – and we know how he shared that relish and knowledge wherever he could.

Of course, a young Ted Ellis, destined to become the People's Naturalist in Norfolk during the second half of the 20th century, was Arthur's keenest disciple. "He hath eyes of a falcon and the optimism of a Sancho Panza" announced his mentor as Ted took the lantern of discovery into another era.

Arthur had many talents, not least in winning the trust of a hard race of men who dominated the Breydon scene, wildfowlers and poachers. Memorable characters like Pintail Thomas Ducker Chambers, Stork Thacker and Short-un Page inspired some of his richest compositions. He also loved the humour and colour of our local dialect and cheered the pages of the Yarmouth Mercury for many years with Melinda Twaddles' Notions. Older readers still recalled and chuckled over those columns when I worked on the Mercury as a young reporter in the 1960s.

The real quality to leap from these pages is a desire to know more about the man, to read as much as possible of his prodigious output and to look closer at the natural world he loved and lauded.

Perhaps modern Yarmouth, facing difficult challenges – social and economic – might do well to seek inspiration from one of its brightest sons.

Watching his sun rise or go down over Breydon is a useful starting-point in any revival programme.

Keith Skipper, Cromer, 2004

INTRODUCTION

Arthur Patterson was born in 1857 in a Yarmouth Row. At the age of three his mother died of tuberculosis, and his father remarried. He was the only child of eight to survive beyond the age of 21, and he believed his intense love of wandering in the open saved him from joining them in the churchyard!

His love of nature began on his father's allotment garden, on the seashore, and on the banks of Breydon Water where he met and gained the trust of a race of men who earned their living from the estuary – wildfowlers and poachers.

Arthur's schooldays were spent at a Primitive Methodist Day School, where he learned the three 'R's from William Wallis, a teacher who encouraged composition, music, singing, drawing and nature study. He started his first nature notebook in 1878 and in the same year contributed his first article to a newspaper. He married Alice Paston, his school sweetheart, and worked at a variety of jobs to meet his family obligations; peddling tea, as an assurance agent, taxidermist, a sewing machine salesman, postman, ticket attendant, zoo-keeper and warehouseman. His first regular employment came in 1892 when he was appointed School Attendance Officer, a post he held for twenty years.

He started writing under the pen-name "John Knowlittle" at the age of 39, at which point he changed his gun for field-glasses. Through his diligent research and observation, he doubled the number of species of fish on the Yarmouth list and added to the Norfolk list; and he increased the knowledge of the habits of gulls and waders, as well as rare visitors to Yarmouth like the spoonbill and avocet, for which his efforts were recognised by the Norfolk and Norwich Naturalists Society. As well as writing books about the wildlife of Breydon, he wrote countless articles for newspapers and nature journals, and gave talks illustrated by lightning sketches. Other leisure hours were spent on voyages into Broadland in a variety of boats, and always meticulously logged for the next book.

In May 1935, he realised his greatest ambition, that of being elected an Associate of the Linnaean Society of London, which was restricted to only 25 associates; his name had been put forward by Her Grace the Duchess of Bedford 29 years earlier in 1906. Arthur Patterson died later that year at the age of 78.

My great-grandmother was a tolerant wife; Arthur once said: "A naturalist's wife has to put up with a great deal of discomfort, but Mrs. Patterson got used to all these things, save nasty - sometime forgotten and what was worse to her – dirty handkerchiefs in which I carried many odd things, from live birds to dead snakes, and living natterjacks to putrid fishes picked up on the seashore. However, I always put family first, and hobby afterwards."

My first book, *John Knowlittle*, published in 1985, told the life of my great-grandfather. This book is an edited collection of scribblings he made in and around Yarmouth. Throughout the book Arthur Patterson's notes are shown in seriphed typeface; my contributions are in non-seriphed typeface. The late Ted Ellis said to me in 1985: "Always leave something in the locker for another time." This collection barely lifts the lid!

Beryl Tooley,
October 2004

Chapter 1
HUMBLE BEGINNINGS

"My mother died when I was not yet four years old - a weary, good woman."

Arthur wrote some autobiographical reminiscences in 1916, in which he vividly described his childhood in the 1860s in Great Yarmouth.

I was born in a humble cottage, numbered 8, in Row 36, then known as the Garden Row, where a few front yards of flowers brightened the outlook. Our cottage was a small one; and herein there were born my several brothers and sisters, of which I am the only one surviving.

Birthplace of Arthur Patterson, Number 8,
Row 36 called "Garden Row" because some
of the houses had little gardens in front of them.

My birth dates back to October 19th, 1857. Some of my brothers and sisters died early. (Arthur was the only child of William and Mary to live beyond the age of 21). As to myself, I was known as the "little pitman," an expression that really appertains to the smallest *sus* in a litter.

Father looked upon diseases, and distresses, as "sent of the Lord" for chastisement, correction, and our edification. He had a very strong will, took most matters philosophically, and outwardly accepted ills calmly. He was as straight as a palm tree, and about as narrow. He rarely laughed. He lived a life of religious travail, but he was honest. At 80 he assured me he could not reckon me up - my love of rambling the marshes, slipping about Breydon, and with a gun, caused him many regrets and worries.

Father was by trade a shoemaker. With him "cobbler's wax" was sufficiently monotonous to suggest to him a higher ambition than cordwaining; and he dearly loved gossiping with chapel-folk of the old and rather bigoted type. If he gossiped over the half-door of a brother "snob" for the half of the day, he made it up by robbing his bedtime hours. In later life he became an insurance agent.

The Patterson family on Yarmouth Beach, 1860.
Arthur is seated on his father's lap, with his sister Mary and brother William

My mother died when I was not yet four years old of tuberculosis - a weary, good woman. Father's second wife was a strapping widow, who had a broad hand, and occasionally corrected me with it. The more I yelled, she said I'd have the more! She ran a little tuck-shop, or humble grocery; and I became an errand boy, taking out the loaves of bread to customers at a distance. One loaf I left daily at the Tolhouse Jail for the janitor, who was a big sulkily-looking man clad in a long black gown, with a sort of rope round his extensive "corporation", that held a big bunch of bright-jingling keys.

As to my ancestors, I know very little, but I gathered from my father that *his* father was a shoemaker, living in a little rural cottage, near the site of the old Post Office at the top of Prince of Wales Road, Norwich. My granddad made shoes for the Fair people, and the *Queen of the Gypsies.* He was also the first man to kick against Norwich Church Rates; but in spite of this, he was made a churchwarden in his parish. My great grandfather, I was told, was an old Highlander who fought under General Wolfe at Quebec going through the Campaign without a scratch. After the War, he had settled in King's Lynn, and from thence wandered to Norwich, where he became a city paver; my father contended when he died in Norwich, the City still owed him over £100. He was placed in his coffin with a parcel of snuff and his favourite drinks.

My stepmother was the widow of a naval man, a peaceable man; nor did he retaliate after she had, in a fit, thrown a bucket at his head, so I understand. Hers was a small shop that sold a variety of small groceries, snuff, tobacco, bloaters and crabs. Her irritability did not affect the dinner hour; and she lavishly fed me, thanks to her Methodist leanings. Father visited the cemetery on Sunday afternoons after the lessons, a favourite walk of his and other Sunday School teachers, discussing religious matters as they trod. I delighted in playing with snails, beetles, woodlice, and any creature that I might find, and handle, and take home specimens wrapped in my handkerchief. Whenever I managed to get an hour or so in the churchyard, I slipped away from the house, and revelled among the yellow dandelions and the crawling caterpillars among the ranker weeds.

From child-hood I was carried, then walked to chapel; and I rather liked the lively preaching, and livelier singing; over-many functions rather wearied me until I was well into my teens. We youngsters, I think, were rather "close hauled", and I give below the orders of the Sunday. No wonder we became not only irritable but also rebellious:

7	a.m.	Morning prayer meeting
9.30	a.m.	Sunday School
10.30	a.m.	Sermon in the chapel
2.30	p.m.	School prayer meeting
6	a.m.	Preliminary prayer meeting
6.30	p.m.	Service at chapel
8 - 9	p.m.	Prayer Meeting again

A coal cart used to transport worshippers to Camp meetings
further afield. Arthur and his Stepmother enjoyed these outings

My stepmother was extremely fond of Camp meetings; so was I and every year we strode across the gorse-smothered sand-hills, which, like the marram grass, grew densely thick, and tall, spreading right away from the Workhouse (Infirmary) Wall to Caister-on-Sea. Not a brick had been laid in the (18)60s, and the only objects between the sea and the (then) dense long line of fir-trees that bordered the length of Caister Road, were the North Star battery, armed with noisy cannons; a post-mill; and the Reserved Gunners' Shed which showed above the gorse. Sinuous tracks for single pedestrians allowed a careful walk for some three miles. It was delightfully wild; stonechats, whinchats, redbacked-shrikes, skylarks, wheatears, turtle-doves and two species of partridges - the English and French - gave a charm to those Denes (or Dunes). My stepmother, too, who was fond of animals and birds, revelled in the sweetness borne on the wind. Occasionally an outing on the Sunday to further villages was engineered by the lady; our pony trotted at its own pace, and our attendance at the "meeting'" was not so lengthy as when kept in town.

My stepmother shut me up on Saturdays (save for errands) when she considered I had "been naughty" during the week; and inflicted on me the indignity of being punished by learning the 23rd Psalm. I could *not* recite it all, and I never could commit to memory to this day. It was a cruel punishment for a sensitive kiddie like myself to be punished. But I could tell her much about Behemoth and other beasts quoted in the Bible.

As stern and dogmatic as my father was, he never used an oath, utterly tabooed medicine, was a total abstainer for 70 odd years, never killed a fly; nor a chicken, which died of old age. A gun he detested and river and salt-water also. As to whether he was right in forbidding me play, or correct in dosing me on the Sunday, I make no comment.

When at Sunday School I eased the monotony by picking out Eastern stories of Daniel and his lions; the ostrich that had its head in the sand; the dove that returned to Noah's ark, and locusts that blighted the earth. I dug out the texts, and pencilled them in the flyleaf of various bibles, as we removed from class to class, but we usually forgot the continuation of the verses.

My father died in 1909, aged 91; he survived his third wife, after 10 years of tyranny over the Old Man, and his great regret was that I prevented him from acting foolishly and annexing another. As it was, his third wife was an old ogre of a woman, with a man's voice, and the occupation of a pickpocket. Her relatives collared everything, except an empty safe and an old umbrella. Father's bankbook was a lean one, the third lady having (to the disgust even of her brother) taken two cottages as well. Her ambition was to have a motorcar; but Beelzebub got his fist in first. Her reward awaited her!

At 8, or thereabouts, I was delighted to get to father's allotment garden at Runham Vauxhall.

Big cabbages fed various caterpillars; other insects buzzed and flew among the flowerbeds. Behind the shed was a clean, crowded ditch of tall reeds, wherein father dipped his water-pot; there whirligig beetles gyrated in the clear bit of water, and marsh prawns, great water beetles, frogs and sticklebacks. Strange larvae wriggled among the duckweed, in particular the rat-tailed maggot and leeches, and dragonflies haunted the reed-tops and the tall grasses. A dead rat, blown with putrefaction, gave me my first wonderings as to the beginnings of life and the endings of it.

I went through the gamut of boyhood's experiments. A menagerie had visited the town, and lions roared, and hyenas laughed. This started me off for a menagerie: I scooped out the insides of corks, and put in a half circle of pins, to represent dens; and I went so far as to shorten flies' wings to see how the clipping affected the losers. My stepmother caught me at it, and after a handful of punishment, she prophesied I would live to be hanged! My gladdest hours were spent with bottles and nets, as well as newts and sticklebacks; but the accumulations of mud and thickened-water brought me into trouble with Lady No. 2; for the drying as I made for home, intensified my pains and well-bedaubed garments.

Today, as rows of pretty and flimsy dwelling-houses are creeping towards Caister, the two miles of ditches have all gone and the firs that bordered each side of the road. In those rows of trees gold-crested wrens, and several other species of arboreal birds, nested. Like the rest of wandering boys, I caught bees, and popped them into separate bottles, hoping they would evacuate a trifle of honey: some of my school-chums robbed mulberry-trees for leaves to feed silkworms, which, in the sixties, were a widespread hobby. An uncle of mine fixed up machinery, and wound the silk into hanks. Young and old were keen on the creatures.

Like the plebeian boys of my early acquaintance, I must need go down to the river-side with a bit of string and weight, and a far-gone mackerel, to catch crabs - the shore-crab. But the ditch that ran along near the foot of the fir trees was my favourite "trawling-ground." Father and his wife dealt with this piscatorial outbreak with suitable words.

Chapter 2
SCHOOLDAYS

*"All the education I got was under Wallis; the polish I got afterwards
by years of grind."*

No man, I think, makes more impression upon the life of a boy than does his schoolmaster; and I am sure the handling of myself by my late dear old schoolmaster, Mr. William Wallis, made more impression upon me, physically, and in my love of the open air, than did my father, who never once laid a finger on me, which Wallis did, often with several fingers clutching a lusty cane. Perhaps I deserved it, and got the more by contortioning my body.

Arthur Patterson was recalling his schooldays in the 1860s in an article for the Eastern Daily Press on December 22nd, 1927.

I spent the earliest of my years at an old Dame's School. I can remember my dreadful anger, when at 3, my locks were shorn by the little fat George Street barber and the terror that made me squirm when my poor sister lugged me, kicking and uproarious, to this old Dame's School. It was in the Glasshouse Row in a quaint old cottage - one of three with a sort of doubly bent roof. The Dame, Mrs. Mutton, had eyes of a kestrel, and promptly seized upon every farthing she saw us twiddling about. These small amateur *crèches* were a Godsend to the poorer parents. The *tuppence* paid the old Dame's rent, and the small folk were as safely folded and housed, as are prize rabbits, sheep and whippets. Sitting on forms we picked up the alphabet in good time, and squawked and snivelled to our hearts' content.

As soon as I had learnt my alphabet, and could be trusted alone, I was taken to the Primitive Methodists' Day School, and duly initiated as a promising pupil. Mr. Wallis, our schoolmaster, came to Yarmouth from Wootton Basset, Wiltshire, in the early 1860's, a small active man, all nerves and go; and he needed them, for the old Day School on Priory Plain, at that period, was very badly equipped. Costing 3d. a day, the School was crowded. We boys on his advent lined up - I was third boy - like raw recruits to welcome him (at his command), and he summarily examined us in mental arithmetic, in which I never especially shone in money problems.

Arthur's School on Priory Plain, Great Yarmouth. At the age of 15 he was appointed Pupil Teacher under Wallis for five shillings a week. Building of the Temple next door commenced in 1874; it replaced the old Primitive Methodist Tabernacle.

What an unkempt crew we were, save those who used hair oil. We used slates, many of them frameless, and some like broken windowpanes. New slates were horrible. We summed on slates and on Thursday afternoons had drawing lessons. How we cleaned them; I know our sleeves polished them. We had monitors; some nice, some hateful. When we were eligible, we had ink and copybooks with stereo headings, for example America was discovered by Columbus. Oh, the poverty of the apparatus that he inherited for tools!

Best of all were the desks, which were double-sided - the girls with many curly ringlets and bare of arm, sat on one slope, we boys sat or jiffled opposite. This was ripping! The girls kicked under the desks; the boys returned the compliment. Duels of grimaces were frequent, alluring smiles as well, and we wrote and delivered messages under them. The future Mrs. Patterson, aged 9, always sat opposite me, when she won in a scramble for the seat. I at 10 exchanged messages written on fragments of foolscap under the desk. In due time I put a ring on her finger. She was a Paston, of the Caister Castle Pastons, of whom Old Henry VIII robbed the rightful owners. There is something in breeding: and my wife was a refined, though poor lady. Whatever my troubles, she cheered me. A naturalist's wife has to put up with a great deal of discomfort, unless she buckles down to it, such as ordinary, sensible men's wives dream not of. But my wife got used to all these things, save nasty, sometime forgotten - and what was worse to her - dirty handkerchiefs in which I carried many odd things from live birds to dead snakes, and living natterjacks and putrid fishes picked up on the seashore.

Mrs. Patterson, pictured with my father in 1914.
Arthur and Alice Elizabeth Paston were married at the Temple on February 5, 1880.
His wages as a relief postman were sixteen shillings a week.

For years good old William Wallis was my only schoolmaster, save for a year under another, while we babbled at "twice times twelve is two dozen". New Irish *"Readers"* were to me most interesting. One chapter dealt with the German snail-gardens, and so impressed me that I gathered up splines of wood and sundry, and made a pen of it. Handfuls of cabbage-leaves were put in for them to feed upon; but I forgot to cover in the top. I had quite a little regiment of them. When father came to the garden next day he was astounded by the number of snails he saw creeping all about the place. These I had collected in some numbers, and let them crawl into the other gardens.

To this mean threepenny day school came Wallis, whose heart at sight of it, sank into his boots. He had no teachers, but at once appointed monitors in turn. Somehow, by Herculean efforts, he reduced things to a system, and soaked us well in the three Rs, and we boys wrote better spelling than even many secondary schools turn out today.

The school exhibitions, with our pencil sketches lining the walls, drew crowds, and the concerts we gave held them. Wallis revelled in music and song, much of which I hum to this day. I was corner-man tenor until my voice broke, when Wallis, in his pert way, pushed me behind the curtains, describing my efforts like those of a duck swallowing hot potatoes. He never could rub *Euclid* or music into me - the comb and tissue paper was the only instrument I could play.

Friday was leisure day. If wet, we had games, and I had to mount a stool and lightning sketch to amuse the kiddies on the board. On fine spring to Autumn Friday afternoons Mr Wallis took us on rambles among the acres of gorse then smothering the North Denes, or to Mautby by the marshes or to Burgh Castle. We trailed home like a lost army, often into the dark of approaching night. We liked Fridays; although having paid the fee it mattered little to many parents how often we truanted. One afternoon we boys raided a field of swede turnips, taking many prisoners. The farmer caught us and lined us up, counted swedes and told our master he must pay a penny for each or go up to "The Horl (Hall)." He paid.

He taught us to love the wild flowers and sights of the country. Taking him for all in all he was a splendid little man, both patient and impatient, and richly deserved the promotions which came along, and the happy old age which he still so much enjoyed. He was rarely ailing, and kept up his botanical rambles almost until the end.

Not a few old boys still live to revere his memory. Many turned out good businessmen - some made their pile. One boy, with all his efforts, never laid the foundation of one. Arithmetic was his bugbear, but he has had great reason to bless the work and patience of one whom we shall see no more.

Chapter 3
BITS OF OLD-TIME YARMOUTH

"There wasn't a house upon the Denes; the railway wasn't thought of."

Arthur wrote a series of articles in the *Yarmouth Mercury* in 1929 recalling his childhood in Yarmouth in the 1860s and 1870s. In them he describes parts of the town and the characters that lived and traded there.

I cannot get away yet from the juvenile years which I spent in and round what was Slum Area, in North Howard Street, until I was fourteen, and so had become well permeated with the atmosphere and every-day life of the then Charlotte Street. We will start from Lacon's Brewery. The ugly old mansion, grimy and battered in its later years, was razed to the ground whilst I was still a youth. I rarely passed the high wall that superseded this barrier from the public, but I recalled the row of jolly old "brewery men," as far as their corpulence was visible, who lolled against the wall, complacently smoking their soot-coloured tobacco pipes and awaiting the stroke of the clock to waddle back to their duties.

An odd old fellow, Freeman by name, who was a corn chandler, with a big red chin and a floury hat, and a toothless mouth that showed a wide-open gape, ran the shop next to Lacon's for years. Further on stands a fine flint-fronted furniture shop, whose flints are as smoothly joined together as any sixteenth century builder could have wished. Then came James Patterson, my uncle, a shoemaker, whose hobby was a Runham allotment, and an almost never-ending couple of pigs, which were fed thrice a day, one hod of swill at eight, and two others later which were worked by a grandfather clock, that by a complexity of brass wheels and strings, emptied the inverted "hods" into the troughs, one a time. Uncle was as proud of - and lucky with - this machinery as an old girl of uncertain age, who had a little stall at Burroughs' Corner, where she sold to kiddies, off to school, several sugar-drops on a bit of cardboard the size of a playing-card, six for a farthing or halfpenny, cut into squares by the scissors.

A few yards off, old Johnson, inventor and vendor of "Johnson's Lick" (which I never "hankered" after) had a dirty-looking canvas tent where he ran the first crude photographs of that period. Next is St. Nicholas Church.

We had really queer shop folk of that day. In a little "tuck" and "tater" shop, the mistress sold herring pickled in vinegar, in season, from a counter-end. A brightly polished brass gas-pipe, with the said herring deep dish, gave out a half-moon shaped naked gas lamp. Flies, at night, were fascinated with the bat's-wing flare, and after a waltz, perhaps giddy as well, they fell into the vinegar, and you could hardly distinguish them as they lay beside the dead herrings. A person of the period never bothered, for the flies greatly resembled whole peppers!

Close by, a shop-lady sold tallow candles, all on string or rush, something like a bunch of very straight bananas. I have seen these candles hung near the ceiling, with rows of "eights" (malt-house candles) and thinner ones, in bunches which dripped tallow drops from the heat above, I can vouch for this because I helped as a little errand boy. They sold coals in stones and half-stones for the very poorest, stored into square boxes up a corner, with derelict meat-covers. Wicked boys with a bent stick not infrequently hauled halfway up the piled two penn'orths, and pulled them down with a crash. That I know is correct, for I helped the miscellaneous lady to reload the boxes. Next to Uncle's we had a Mr. Cooper, shoemaker and bird-catcher, who introduced "paraffin" (so early named) at 7d. a pint, then 6d. and so on. Quite a miscellany vendor.

Next we call up Joe Wilshak, who was a very plump watchmaker. He was a Volunteer and seemed so proud of his then clumsy rifle, that he came to the shop door to clean it, alternating with oil outside the barrel, and a brightness of steel inside that called for admiration. Joe's father, who preceded him, almost everlastingly sat on his seat, until he reminded me of a full flour-sack. Wilshak senior lived next door to my stepmother; he ran a very small grocery shop too. He detested her grey parrot because it was not only a fluent talker, but also a terrible blackguard. Let me tell a story of it.

My Stepmother taught Polly to whistle Ranter's Hymns, and among these snatches of violent poetry was this chorus:

> *Sweet Beaulah land, sweet Beaulah land,*
> *As on the highest mount I stand;*
> *I look away across the sea,*
> *Where mansions are prepared for me,*
> *I view the bright and glorious shore,*
> *My heaven, my home, for evermore.*

Arthur and Polly, the parrot, who bit the
young boy like an alligator, given the chance.
He is dressed in a suit made by his stepmother.

Stepmother and Polly became ecstatic and rattled these verses off as if steam-engined. Polly rasped the cage wires, danced on her perch, swore; yes, actually, swore. Old Wilshak next door detested her; he fumed at intervals, more because of the laughter that rollicked in front of the shop. Polly shrieked, and so did the audience. She blew nosey noises, she flapped her wings; and stepmother hung the cage outside to get a bit of peace indoors. When she - the bird - got warmed up again she nodded her head to the tune of *Polly put the kettle on and we'll all take tea* - and usually interspersed with expletives!

Worse than all happened when the then busier, worse-paid, Methodist clerics called on their visits to pray, Polly cranked up, and so roisterously, that during prayer Step-mother would chuck off her apron, and whack the cage, and so viciously, that the parson shortened his ministrations, and bolted. After that shocked clerics seemed to shun the haunted house. Polly lived to a grand old age.

There is a story told of a bereaved lady that had a pet parrot, which to her sorrow, died. She scoured the bird shops and found them all but one sold. The ornithologist, who was a barber, bowed. "What can I do for you ma'am?" he asked.

She told, weepingly, of her loss.

"What's that one doing - sold?" she enquired.

"No ma'am, she's the biggest blackguard," he said; "she swore like a trooper. I'd be glad to get ten bob for it."

"Then I'll have it," said she, "it's just what I want. I'll have it; it'll so remind me of my poor husband what's gone before."

In one of the Rows was run a tramps' lodging house, and for the separate brown teapots on the stoves, the droppers-in were plentiful. The spouts now and then were a little short in length. In it dwelt a huge dirty old chap, who was over six foot long and big in bulk. He ambled to the then crowded shipyards and stuffed his bag with shavings, which he sold. He had a "north eye", and a beard much like that of a hand-brush. His boots rarely kept in at the toes. He still lived in the Row, but was not respectful enough for a tramp. He partly emptied his unsold chips and shavings, and got inside the sack for the night, and that in the pump house.

Jack Frost was a notable person who lived in the same Row - several doors off. He was fat and flabby, but happy enough when lifted into the tumbledown dickey-cart. In the seasons he was known for the variety of his wares. He had a "had-been" white, battered, top hat. His hard-working friends lifted him into the carriage. It was a dark blanket, if I am not incorrect, that was wrapped around his loins. Tough string helped the ancient straps and collars to keep the machinery together. And he carried as a whip a scraped and lithy bullock's tail! Fortunately the donkey's ribs had long been hammered by a robust bludgeon, and might almost have served for a blacksmith's hammer. The dickey never complained, never wept, and always seemed "as you were!" In winter Frost sold cockles - in millions; rabbits too. In the usual contents of his cart were mussels, bottled horehound beer and pop. Maybe there's rest in heaven even for long-eared quadrupeds.

In the same Row lived two or three red-herring retailers. Hard-working ladies, they always smelt of "reds", for night and day they vended red herrings. How these hard-slogging ladies kept their heads up has been to me wonderful. For such humble folks as these I have much sympathy and respect.

Then there was little Pat O'Connor, who left Ireland as a trumpet-blower in the Militia; he was short, plump, and quick like his Irish folk. To see him blowing beside the big German's brass monster on the march, straddling his legs to keep step, was a delight for onlookers. O'Connor got a job as sanitary-inspector, which suited him to the ground. How many bad pumps he condemned I cannot say. Taps sprang up like thistles and ousted pump-owners like a plague. I have been told since that under the soil of Yarmouth enormous storage of water has been discovered. But I doubt it; and Breydon mud flats are hardening sufficiently to build bungalows on. You would hardly believe that gaggles of tame geese, half a century ago, swarmed on the denes. They left the vicinity of Stanley Road houses to mooch up and down the Rows, picking up broken bread, herrings, crusts, vegetables and what not, which were thrown on the streets, after which they marched off home to wash and nap. It took our council folks years to oust the geese. Today no geese are in evidence.

The river Yare looking east to Southtown Bridge and Town Hall.

Hard Times

It is difficult to see how much the better wages of today are - as a rule - a set-off against the higher cost of living. In the 60's working folk toiled longer hours, and in many instances, without a doubt worked the more cheerfully, giving their mind to their work, rather than worrying all the week about the next football match and the possible winner of the Derby.

You could then get a 2lb. loaf for two pence, a stale one for a farthing less. Bread was the staple food of the poor. I pay sixpence for mine and do not begrudge it, for it is food and medicine. We bought splendid liver, cut on the butcher's block in the middle of a crowd, for four pence, a saucerful. Today the cost per pound is the old-time price of steak - the doctor's recommendation of it will make it dearer. Tripe in the 60's was sixpence - the whole "bag" (stomach). Prejudice was hot against it for human consumption, and the dogs fed on it. Today folks stand round the stalls on Yarmouth market and devour it openly.

I forget the then price of sugar, real Jamaica sugar, with the cobbles of congealed sugar in it and I believe we gave 8d. for a loaf of "cone" sugar. Dumpling - real light dumpling, minus a pastry rind, was a great penny "dish" as bought at Reade's cook shop in Charlotte Street, and Isaac's on the Church Plain, afterwards Mortlocks. Swimming in rich gravy we hopped home with it, perhaps with six for the family. Real appetising "light dumplins" they were. I used to fetch my own. Tea was dearer, but people used more coffee. Folks had a coffee pot, with a handle as on a pump, and the shape thereof was like a big pepperbox. Pork was cheap. The baker's man came for the dinners, and fetched the homemade loaves; his board would be covered with three layers of tins and dishes. A penny for baking a dinner saved twopen'orth of coals. The bake-house was a public centre. Some folks fetched their dinners and saw to it that they got their own. Ructions occurred when a baked joint went to the wrong house. Some folks quarrelled with the baker because the meat shrank, which was an insinuation. Low tide in the gravy made folks argue the cause of it. Had he "skum" the gravy for greasing the bread tins? Had he added water? Evaporation in a hot public oven needed a little. Now and again a pie-dish broke, or a cracked one gave way. Then the folks argued unkindly.

Vegetables were cheaper. Many poor folk used the markets. Notwithstanding costermongers went round. Some people put their marketing off till late - same as they did the Christmas goose - to get a bargain in pork or mutton - for country folk then had no icebox or a refrigerator. Butter was moulded in a wooden cone, and then turned out, one end being stamped flatter with a wooden swan or a cow, shaped like a London high-flying top. Apples and fruit were measured: butter was "half-pinted." In Cambridge, butter used to be sold by the yard. Much salt butter, excellent stuff, came from Holland in light tubs. Country folk often used burnt chestnut for coffee making.

We had tea and breakfasted in winter by candlelight. At seven pence a bushel we kept the fire going with coke. We had no water rate, for almost every house had a well, or a partable or exclusive pump. Rates, I've heard my father say, were sixpence in the pound, but it must have been in his youth. Gas lamps and electricity were unknown in the poorer houses. A pound of candles lasted, generally, a week.

When I was twelve I met with an adventure. Two of us, cousins, climbed up the church steeple (St Nicholas). One found his way down; I couldn't in the dark, until the bell ringers collected round the bottom open door. So I was rescued! We used to have several whale ships sail out of Yarmouth. The expected launch from the beach at Caister of the Lady Flora, an iron steam ship of 250 feet in length, had incited us to climb up and see her launched. The year was 1869. I have always hated ladders ever since.

Nelson's Monument on the South Denes, Yarmouth,
as it looked in Arthur's childhood. The sand dunes then were
covered with wild flowers, and insects and birdlife were abundant

On May 25th, 1863, I was just old enough to know that a man named Marsh had climbed Nelson's Monument, on the South Denes, and when clambering up the caryatids, carved out of stone, had slipped and fallen headlong to the stony steps, some 140 feet, and was killed.

There was a big fellow known as Hales, the Norfolk giant, who appears to have travelled with showmen. He was born in Somerton in 1820; his height was 7ft. 6ins. and he scaled 33 stone. Chest, waist and boots were well in keeping. A brother measuring 6ft. 5ins. died comparatively young, and another brother was above the normal. I always turned to stare at a rather clumsy brother, whose bent shoulders spoiled the true height of him. A sister of Hales died in Yarmouth Infirmary in March 1874. She stood 6ft. 3ins. and bowed each time she entered the house.

There was a great patch of sand in the heart of the town. The east wall threw its shadow upon it. Sheep, donkeys, twine spinners and net driers used it, and where the late Dr. Mayo's house stands, (St. George's Park House, Alexandra Road), town carts and sundry were planted, the whole making a sorry outlook. The late Mr. Edward Stagg persuaded the Council and the public that the place was just the right spot to make for Yarmouth a nice little park. Instead of running into "thousands", it cost the ratepayers a mere £449. For his good work, two hundred subscribers presented a silver tray to him. After grassing the area, and planting a row or two of rather distorted trees, iron rails were also planted and sheep were installed; but in the end this small park was worth all the trouble and old folks greatly enjoy the quietude and peacefulness.

We had in the town some score and more donkeys who, like our visitors, in summer, mustered up on the sea front and the sands. Most of the "dickeys" grazed on the North Denes, then a great spread of furze bushes covering many acres, that began at Caister and spread their thick bushes and prickles right up to where the M. & G.N. (Midland and Great Northern) Railway bridge now crosses the road. Indeed, one could start at the Workhouse corner and steer north-eastward without seeing a house on one's left. There were rolling hummocks of marram grass right to the Britannia Pier. Then came the building of the New Town (Newtown).

Chapter 4
SOME QUAINT OLD YARMOUTH TRADES

"What a lot of institutions and quaint usages I have seen die out in Yarmouth since I appeared on the scene in 1857."

The following articles are from a series of Arthur's *"Notes and Observations on Decayed Little Industries"* written for the *Eastern Evening News* in 1929.

The Fishwharf
When I was a small boy there was no fishwharf in Yarmouth, and fish were landed on the beach; the May and June mackerel-fishery being, to my mind, the most interesting. Elderly women with trailing skirts, who preceded the advent of the Scotch gypper girls, washed the fish in keelers - tubs big enough to scald a pig in - and packed them in osier-lidded peds, sometimes known as hampers.

The "bullock" boats - great Stockholm-tarred vessels - rowed out to fetch the mackerel; as they did to tranship the great hefty plaice that were piled up in bigger hampers or peds, with the lids arching over the fish, and laced-to. Big plaice are rare today, and mingy little ones turn up, for use in the fry-shops.

"The 'bullock' boat was peculiar to Yarmouth companies," as David Higgins says in his book *The Beachman*. *"It was designed to transfer or 'ferry' the fish from craft anchored offshore to the beach auction area beside the Jetty. Well loaded with packages of fish, they could withstand the buffeting of the breakers and take the hard knocks received while lying alongside the fishing boats. They were usually tarred but some were painted red, others blue. The name "bullock" boat was originally a term of ridicule, which stuck, but as time went by it evolved into the word "bulley". With the demise of fish ferrying, after the opening of Yarmouth Fishwharf in 1869, a number of these boats were bought for general use by the village companies and survived with them well into the twentieth century."*

The making of "peds" and building of troll-carts is no more. So are the barrow carts that were later used in carting the herring swills, motor lorries taking their place. There was a round flattish basket, looking in shape like a huge soup-plate. A hollow in the middle, to hold it on a fish-hawker's head, made a slope inside to lean the soles and whitings upon, spike-fashion.

According to ancient prints, the swills, whose tops are today shaped like a figure 8, made so by the middle binder, or one might say handle, were preceded by a half-round rocker-shape, on a kind of half-moon or crescent pattern, or the half-circular, side-handled cheese-cutter of the 1860s.

When I did the Broads in 1919 I provisioned at Stalham. There stood a small harness-maker's shop, on whose forecourt were scores of stout, lifebuoy-like donkeys' collars, rotting in the rain and sun; probably left there as a reminder of the passing of the ass. Two other Broadland rush articles are now practically, if not quite, extinct - the rush-made lifebuoys (at least in Yarmouth) and the frail basket. There are gone, too, the hand-made candlesticks, some with one, others two or even three holders, with shanks bent to fit on a fish-house baulk, or smaller ones with a short spike that could be tapped in the mortar or in the baulks with a hammer. I sent two to the Bridewell Museum, Norwich, and curiosity hunters got the others. Now electric light is used.

Mackerel

Yarmouth Troll Carts

High up on the list of quaint industries is the old Troll-cart, a vehicle peculiar to "Bloaterville"; and in the old jog-trot days it was exceedingly useful in navigating the Rows, wherein were warehouses and fish-houses too. Troll carts were of three kinds, and varied somewhat in size, the largest being used for cargo stuff landed on the Quay, e.g. tuns of brandy, hogsheads of sugar, and what not, which had been landed by ancient brigs mostly, that had gone through the Straits to the Mediterranean and wallowed and rolled back again across the bay. The trolls were narrow and spring-less, and jolting up and through the stone-cobbled rows was not all joy riding. Troll-carts preceded the long dog, or barrow carts, in racing up the tan road on the beach, north side of the Jetty, with peds of lusty plaice, the mackerel, and the swills of herring that were landed by the "bullock" boats. In the 1860s a small dickey troll-cart and a wizened-up little man (foster brother maybe to the donkey) used to cart away the refuse and shop sweepings from the Broad Row.

"HARRY-CARRY," FROM A CONTEMPORARY PRINT.

The Yarmouth Coach or "Harry-Carry

When Daniel Defoe visited Yarmouth, of which place he was "fond", he rather contemptuously spoke of the "Harry coaches", stating that they were "only wheelbarrows with a horse in them". Great fun they were, for with the wheels so close together they were very unsafe, and given on occasion to an upset. Jack Tar from the fleets in the Yarmouth Roads, out for a spree on shore leave, got his money's worth out of his fare.

Arthur seated on a troll-cart outside the Tolhouse Museum. He bought it in 1902 for 30 shillings, to present to the museum. It had been used by Lacon's brewery to convey casks of beer to Nelson's fleet. It was destroyed in the Tolhouse fire during enemy action in the Second World War. A replica can be seen in the present museum

Old-time Clay Pipes

I would, but cannot, smoke. Without a doubt the wooden briar pipe, with a hold of ample dimensions, has come to stay and to make, for me, torture when a non-smoking compartment is packed with inveterate smokers. Old Laddie Woods, the Gorleston Lifeboat hero, who had come with some chums to the whale show in Norwich Market late one Saturday night, made remark as the crew bundled into the 2 a.m. train on the Sunday morning, *"Now we'll smoke old Patt'son out!"* and they did, for I was giddy enough when we landed at Yarmouth, and reeked of tobacco smoke for a week!

Now for many years clay pipes of a queer shape had been dredged up with the mussels in the North river (Bure), and all way down to the sea, never a complete one, so far as I've seen; and they have been dug up near the riverside gardens and adjacent soil. The riverside folk always looked upon these strong broken-shanked pipes as great curiosities, and wondered much at their finding them, and in such numbers. I have wondered whether they were of the churchwarden length, which averaged some 18 inches in the shank; and that the users on breaking one threw it away. I never remember an old Breydoner using one; and what he did use rarely had more than an inch in the shank. And black were those old du-dees; and what language! if they broke one when afloat. Did the pipe makers throw in broken pipes!

In Yarmouth Tolhouse Museum, we have two cases of these antique pipes, the smaller one shown probably dating back to Charles I period; and a slight variation in lengths and capacities ensued down to the time of William and Mary. James I, I believe, wrote a hot counterblast to tobacco, and folks smoked in secret when this eccentric monarch was around.

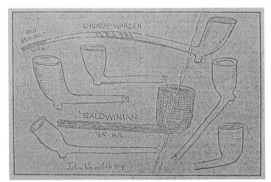

A collection of ancient clay pipes in the Tolhouse Museum

Matches, candles and coffins

"John the Tinker," of 1860, was "John the Matchman" of the '40s. He dipped split sticks both ends in soft sulphur, and sold them for matches, tied in bundles, to those who still used tinderboxes. He sat in the "free" seats in

21

the old Primitive Methodist Tabernacle, always unwashed. On cold Sunday mornings I watched and heard him chafe his hands like sandpaper. He had a bent left leg, which was fitted into a wooden frame, and strapped there, so he seemed to sit at every step, a toe at the end stumped like a peg-leg. He had a face like a squinting demon, or a church gargoyle.

And candles. Who among our thousands of kiddies has seen a tallow candle manufactured? I've watched thousands, for my stepmother kept a little shop - two shops, in her day (55 and 56, Howard Street,) and among cheeses, bread puddings, coals, bread, ha'porths of snuff, penn'orths of tea, sugar, and so on, she sold tallow candles - dips, both cotton and rush-lights, ranging from a ha'penny to a penny each. They hung above the gas (nearly), which kept them warm! They sometimes dripped. I fetched them from Tunbridge's, and I also often peeped in Jackson's where Cooper's stove warehouse now is, with its sombre town wall, arches, and romantic dreams of older days.

To be brief, the candle-dipper was a revolving machine, which worked very much like the ancient rotary bookshelf in St. Nicholas' Church, or better still, in the similitude of the ups-and-downs at the old-time fairs. Each revolution dipped a spit-full of tallowing cotton or rush wicks, thickening and drying at every dip in the trough of boiling, stinking tallow. They were sold on strings like warps of herrings, and then sold in ones or twos. Only maltsters use them today.

A strange man was Matthews, the coffin-maker, of White Horse Plain. He was unclean-looking, fat and squabby, a larger Quilp than Dickens invented. He rang the Curfew bell at 5 a.m. and at 8 p.m. Slopping across the road in his "bursted" slippers, and hair-throat exposed, his apron fluttering like a flag of distress - in all weathers. Some jokers, probably "Putty" Bly, Holiday, the barber, and Grimes, the shoemaker, roused him out one night after twelve, scaring him when they told him it was gone five! Off he bolted up the belfry steps, and scared the town, who mustered, I believe, in hundreds round the church rails.

He contracted for the workhouse coffins, at eight to ten shillings each, I believe. He made them of packing cases, orange boxes and the like. Martha stained them with some yellow ochre. Elijah Mason "overlooked" the pauper funerals. Four old decrepit men - paupers - drove the hearses, which had no springs, some four wheels and four shafts sticking out of the sides, which the ancients shoved along painfully. "Lower her gently, Elijah!" was Matthew's caution. Once the old chaps, fitter to be inside the elongated baker-like barrow than pushing it, let a coffin slip, when the poor thing inside pushed the end out with its feet. Old men if not feeble are often awkward.

Chapter 5
THE FIRST SCRIBBLINGS OF A NATURALIST

"I think it was in 1864 that my stepmother relented a bit, and started me off with "Chatterbox", that favourite periodical of a bygone age."

Having acquired a taste for an animal book, Arthur saved halfpennies until he had two pence and bought a small book entitled *"Gleanings in Nature History,"* which held in its pages a Lion and Elephant and a very mixed menagerie. He wrote:

The little volume stirred up my nature-instincts, more than any book I ever bought, or wrote.

In a benevolent moment, Stepmother gave me a volume by the Rev. Houghton, as a birthday present. This added fuel to fire, and I read it over and over again. Its coloured plates, more especially depicting the dog capturing salmon, fascinated me. Fired by this, I quickly learnt to find marine curiosities, e.g. starfishes, curious crabs and what not, whose names I had to puzzle out on my own initiative. The first fish that I captured alive was a very small flounder, which I carried home between two oyster-shells. If I remember rightly, I had some difficulty in giving it a name. Since then I have been enraptured with Breydon, and the flounders I have caught there and had fried for my dinner.

At that period we had ridges of sand cliffs; and tons of flint stones rolling, and gathering, as the sea-waves rolled them up the beach. These gathered the blown sands and marrams held them, and piled the sand dunes around them. Then the Wise Men of Yarmouth sent herds of "out-of-works" to collect them, and cart them to handy *holls*, where hammers broke them to pieces for road making! (What a contrast against our tar-built roads!) This loss of resistance swept the tides continuously higher. And the north-east winds *laved* the tall sand cliffs, and the tides joined in the segregation. Hence we get very little seaweed at the tidemark nowadays, the tides are more rapid, and few marine creatures come ashore on Yarmouth beach.

By about 1867, Arthur had built up quite a library according to the list that follows. Believed to be his earliest writing, the list is bound into *"Fancy 3"*, a collection of boyhood pamphlets.

Natural History
Common Objects of the Seashore
Fancy 1, 2, 3, 4, 5
Woods Natural History
Popular Natural History
Zoology for Schools
Architecture of Birds
Insect Miscellanies
The Observing Eye
What is a Bird?
British Birds
Little Library Birds
White's Selborne
Bingleys Tales about Birds
Seaside Lesson Book
Wonders of the animal kingdom
Baffon's Natural History
Ingpen's Entomologists Guide
The Marine Aquarium
Natural History Book
From January to December
The Orders of Insects
The Orders of Butterflies
The Handbook of Fowls
Lloyd's Natural History of
  Butterflies
A visit to the Zoo
Poultry Books
Insects Changes
British Butterflies
Cage Birds
My first Birdie Book
Zoology

Books of Adventure
Robinson Crusoe
Swiss Family Robinson
A Boy's Adventures in Australia
Under the Gum Tree
The Swan and her Crew

Geographical
Goldsmith's Popular Geography
Recreation in Physical Geography

History
The Brave Boys of Derry
The Heroic Reader History of
  England
Old Stories from British Isles
New Historical Readers
English History

Odds
Stories for Summer Days and Winter
  Nights
The Rocket
Months and Seasons
Penny Readings
Readings and Recitations
Wonders of the World
Holidays at Wilton
Ready Reckoner
Johnson's Dictionary of the English
  Language

At the age of 21, Arthur wrote his first Natural History paragraph, in the shape of a letter about kingfishers, to the *"Standard"*. His second article on November 13th the same year, on the subject of late swallows, was the first of countless he went on to write for the *Eastern Daily Press*. Thrilled at seeing his letters in print he bought a book and pasted them inside. This was the first of his nature diaries. Every article he wrote to a newspaper or journal was cut out and methodically pasted into his diaries, together with sequential replies from correspondents, odd letters, nature notes, drawings, and so on.

TO THE EDITOR OF THE STANDARD.

Sir,—With considerable pleasure, doubtless with many others, I read in your paper of the 16th the letter of "A Serpentine Bather," in which he speaks of having seen a kingfisher in the very heart of London. Without doubt it is very rare in that vicinity, but down here, in Norfolk, this bird is become quite common. In Yarmouth they seem of late to have been very plentiful. This month and last I have seen as many as half a dozen before breakfast when taking a lengthy stroll by the River Bure and the adjacent marshes. From what I can make out the proportion is five young birds to every two old ones seen or shot. A young man, on the 17th inst., shot one old bird and four not in full plumage. What a pity it is that such indiscriminate slaughter should be made upon these handsome birds, so pleasing to the naturalist, and whose history is so full of interest. Bird-stuffers here give but fourpence and sixpence for these little bird-gems, according to the richness of their plumage.

A circumstance has just come under my own notice, which I beg leave to give. A friend of mine was out shooting by the Bure yesterday (17th) when he heard the cry of a whimbrel, or half-curlew (*Numenius phœopus*). He whistled it, and it flew circling like a pigeon in great agitation, and with a sharp curve alighted upon the roof of a house on the other side of the river, beyond gunshot, where for several minutes it rested. I have never heard of a wading-bird doing so before.

This summer two pairs of swallows built in the hold of an old ship, lying in the centre of 200 acres of salt water, known as Breydon Water, where it is partly sunken to act as a breakwater to a "drain." Several feet of water are in the hold, yet the birds have succeeded in bringing off several young ones, which now fly about with them.

I am, Sir, your obedient servant,

A YOUNG NATURALIST.

22, Caistor-road, Great Yarmouth, September 18.

Arthur's first published letter

To the Editor of *The Standard,* September 19th, 1878

SIR- With considerable pleasure, doubtless with many others, I read in your paper of the 16th the letter of *"A Serpentine Bather,"* in which he speaks of having seen a kingfisher in the very heart of London. Without doubt it is very rare in that vicinity, but down here, in Norfolk, this bird is become quite common. In Yarmouth they seem of late to have been very plentiful. This month and last I have seen as many as half a dozen before breakfast when taking a lengthy stroll by the River Bure and the adjacent marshes. From what I can make out the proportion are five young birds to every two old ones seen or shot. A young man, on the 17th, shot one old bird and four not in full plumage. What a pity it is that such indiscriminate slaughter should be made upon these handsome birds, so pleasing to the naturalist, and whose history is so full of interest. Bird-stuffers here give but four pence and

25

sixpence for these little bird-gems, according to the richness of their plumage.

A circumstance has just come under my own notice, which I beg leave to give. A friend of mine was out shooting by the River Bure yesterday when he heard the cry of a whimbrel, or half-curlew *(Numenius phoepus)*. He whistled it, and it flew circling like a pigeon in great agitation, and with a sharp curve alighted upon the roof of a house on the other side of the river, beyond gunshot, where for several minutes it rested. I have never heard of a wading bird doing so before.

This summer two pairs of swallows built in the hold of an old ship, lying in the centre of 200 acres of salt water, known as Breydon Water, where it is partly sunken to act as a breakwater to a "drain." Several feet of water are in the hold, yet the birds have succeeded in bringing off several young ones, which now fly about with them.

I am, Sir, your obedient servant, A YOUNG NATURALIST.

22 Caister Road, Great Yarmouth, September 18th.

Swallows, 1907

To the Editor of the *Eastern Daily Press*, November 14th, 1878.

Late Swallows

SIR - I read with pleasure the letter of your correspondent, James Wilson, in your issue of the 13th, in which he speaks of having seen so recently "quite a number of swallows (house-martins) flying about". This autumn, here in Yarmouth, has been an unfavourable one for observations on the summer migrants, and the birds alluded to above seem to have flitted earlier than is usual. I find among my rough "bird notes", an entry to this effect, which was penned last year:

"November 5th, 1877, saw a pair of swallows (*Hirundo urbica*) this fine open morning, flying about over the refuse-pits of the town. From whence had they come?"

In reference to this note I would say, for several days I had lost sight of them, but on that day two made their appearance, and were, as the gentleman says, "still behaving in all respects as if it had been a summer day". It puzzled dear old Gilbert White to account for their sudden appearance after intervals of absence, and it puzzles me.

Thanking James Wilson for his note, and apologising for trespassing so much upon your space.

I remain, yours, A YOUNG NATURALIST.

His first newspaper contribution to a Yarmouth newspaper did not appear until September 25th, 1880. It related to the "Solitary Snipe", sometimes called the great or double snipe.

He recorded that on December 4th, 1880 he received his first naturalist's letter; it was from Mr. John Henry Gurney, F.L.S., F.Z.S., of Keswick Hall, Norwich, one time president of the Norfolk and Norwich Naturalists' Society, and annual contributor of Bird Notes to the *"Zoologist"*.

Arthur with James Beckett, 1887. The two naturalists shared an interest in microscopy. Beckett became a journalist for the Eastern Daily Press

By the First World War, Arthur had been writing a nature journal for thirty-six years. In January 1918 a fragment of a German bomb slightly damaged his home. Not wishing to see his life's work destroyed, he decided to place in Norwich Public Library for safe keeping his manuscript notebooks, original articles and letters, a complete set of his cartoons, drawings and a set of his published books. He wrote in his diary:

Having received an intimation from the Germans - in the shape of a fancy brick smashed by them last Monday, 10 inches below my bedroom window - besides other unkind visits from them when on the water - I have considered it only right that my life's work should not be 'bust up' whatever they may or may not do to me.

In response to these new acquisitions, George A Stephen, F.L.A., City Librarian, produced a Reader's Guide in July 1918 (Vol. VII, No. 3) prefaced by a short biography.

"In February, the City Council passed a vote of thanks to this eminent Norfolk naturalist for his gift, on certain conditions, of all his notebooks from 1878 to date, a complete set of his published books, articles and letters, and complete set of his local and other cartoons. He decided to offer his collection to Norwich because, to use his own words, 'Norwich is the intellectual centre of Norfolk, my father and grandfather were Norwich citizens, and I have received many sincere and unsolicited kindnesses at the hands of Norwich and county people - the naturalists of Norfolk and Norwich in particular.'
"In 1878 be began his long series of notebooks, in which he recorded day by day his careful observations of the fauna, preserved notes of curious and interesting specimens which have been brought to him, pen and ink sketches and coloured drawings of interesting examples, and letters from other naturalists relating to his work. These journals are thus a mine of valuable information and are probably more extensive than those of any other Norfolk naturalist. Fortunately much of their contents has been published, for Mr Patterson is a prolific writer... His first book appeared serially in the "Yarmouth Gazette", *and it was issued in book form in 1887, with the title* "Sea-side Scribblings for Visitors".*
"An amateur artist of no mean ability, Mr Patterson has illustrated some of his books, and he has won for himself a reputation as a local cartoonist. He has standing to his credit well over a thousand effective cartoons relating to politics, football, and angling, which achieved great popularity. His ability is well shown in sixty cartoons entitled "Humours of Norfolk History", *which were published in the* "Norwich Mercury" *series of newspapers, a number of cartoons on* "Humours of Angling", *published in the* "Anglers' News", *and in the hundreds of cartoons published in the* "Yarmouth Mercury" *between the years 1897 - 1914.*

"It is generally a moot point whether the works of authors of modern creative literature will 'live' or not, but there can be no doubt that Mr. Patterson's work as a naturalist will endure. His extensive records will be as highly valued by future naturalists as they are by those of today. His work has received unstinted praise by many British naturalists, to whom Yarmouth connotes Patterson, and more than once it has been said that the mantle of Gilbert White of Selborne has fallen on him."

This last comment must have pleased him, for Gilbert White had been one of his childhood heroes and his book, *The Natural History of Selborne,* inspired him from his youth.

After Arthur died in 1935, my great-uncles deposited all of their father's manuscripts at the Norfolk Record Office. These and those Arthur had, himself, in 1918, deposited there, are now preserved in the Norfolk Record Office at the Archive Centre, Martineau Lane, Norwich. I am indebted to the Archive staff for their help with my research both for *John Knowlittle*, the biography of my great-grandfather, in 1985, and for this publication.

A Mercury Cartoon topical for the day. The caption read as follows: "The Council, in solemn conclave, discussed bullocks; and directed the Chief-constable to instruct his officers to stop any cattle being driven up Regent Street at 9 a.m. But Alderman Whelk (who represents the Council) had not made provision against any of the said cattle coming down the street, hence the result!" - Yarmouth Roarer, May 14, 1898.

Carnival Day, 1898. Arthur, right, is advertising the Mercury Cartoons and Melinda Twaddles' Notions, imaginary stories written in the local dialect. Picture from a glass slide courtesy of Peter Allard.

Melinda Twaddles' Notions
(written during the First World War)

Good Friday Episodes

Well, frinds, I often think that if we know'd all what we eat, we wouldn't eat at all, my mother useter say to father, when she biled the taters not properly eyed.

"Ah, bor, howd yer row," she says, "we all ha' got to eat a peck o'dirt afore we dye; and we mite as well do it fust as larst!"

"Don't tell me, maw," he'd say, " but let me hev things done properly."

Yet he'd eat his fry'd sprats without removin' scales, brains, hearts and livers, and all that; and swaller whilks without takin' the bones out, and sossidge with the skins on.

"I don't want no more of your saffern bungs!" says Mrs. Pigwink to Mrs.Chittleburgh, "they pritty nigh kilt me."

Then in cums Mrs. Ripsaw, and Mrs Popcorn, and says the same thing.

"I'd like to know what you mean, you wimmen," says she; "what's rong? You must hev bin eatin' dry pidgen peas, or caster-ile beans."

"We hopes you aint bin usin arseynick!" gasps Mrs. Pigwink.

"No! My lady," says she, "I've bin using good bakin' powder!" and she brings down 2 tins: one was marked BAKIN POWDER, and the other CARBINETED SODER. She smells, and sniffs, and then she tastes, and turnin' white, sits down on a cheese box, what collapses, and drops her in it.

"Smellin' solts!" she gasps, but we couldn't find it, so we shakes the pepper cruet onder her nose, till she cums round.

"Oh deer!" she gasps, "if I didn't empty the powders in the rong tins!"

We all loox serious; but as none of us hed to get a horsepitel ticket, we presently busts out a-larfin.   No more of her buns for me!

Our Tribunal Again

We – that is, the Golleston Tribuner – met again in Tin Kittle Schole a-Wensday, and Curate Crippen took the cheer. He'd got newralger that bad, you wouldn't think, till his rite cheek was as big as a punkin.   Fortshunately, theer was no objextors, but sum letters cum in, which he reeds.   The first was as follers:-

Sir- I objext to cum to a appeal: I'm a Englishman, and believe in Freedom,. So if you expeckts me this morning – don't. I shell do nothing towards soljerin, bein quite content to go about in woman's clothes. So, if you're still wanting me – find me. I'm not a Brithren. I'm an out and out rank Infidelity, and Free think, as well as Free do.   Yours truly Josiah Whichway

Then one more letter cups up from Colchester

Sir, and Gents – I was a Brithren when I refused to jind (the army), threw Conscientious Objections, but last Monday week I got saved at the Salwation Army, and hev now jined the Field Artillery. I feel a new man !.
                   Yours, Joseph Brown.

Crippen said "Hooray!" and all the committee said "Hooray," and the meetin said "Hooray," and dismist.

Zach rites about our youngest son in Wales who got married last week:

Our new dorter-in-law

Our little Jerry grew to be
A six-fut well bilt man;
He'd corted since he was 4-fut three,
He's plump, and brown with tan,

He's in the Norfik Cycle Corp,
And holds a stripe or two;
And if the enemy's near our shore -
He'll fite for me and you.

He used to hev his dole of sop.
And sucked his little otes;
And now he grows a normous crop of
Tosh beneath his nose.
And she - we've only seen her once
Is fine and fair to see -

Her tout ensemble's plump and nice -
Our dorter-in-lore is she.

Well, let us home for him, and all
The blissed solger boys,
Who've listened to theer Country's Call
And now share wedded joys,

That safe from out this war they'll drop,
And see domestic bliss, -
Of blissed babies hev a crop,
For grandmamma to kiss.

Yours as usurel,
Melinda
Birnt Lain Bungerlow,
Golleston.

Chapter 6
FROM GUN TO BINOCULARS

"I had a gun more to assist studies than kill and a gun was the means whereby I got out at 3 o'clock in the morning after working long hours the day before."

From a very early age, Arthur wanted a gun. The father of one of his school chums, Ben Harwood, took Arthur on his first sail across Breydon, and owned a "sensitive, straight-shooting old gun", which he kept stowed under the forepeak loaded. Unbeknown to Ben, Arthur and Bernie took out his boat, and there Arthur took his first shot. He put the butt to his shoulder, it went off, knocking him into the punt backwards and he had an aching shoulder afterwards. Undeterred Arthur saved enough money to buy a gun, but he was too afraid to take it home, for fear of the wrath of his father and stepmother who strongly disapproved of guns. Another friend, Ben Dye, stored it for him in the bake house where he worked. Ben Dye, who became his lifelong companion, and he went out shooting on the sand dunes, along the river and on Breydon and both had a go at taxidermy to make a little money. Arthur never claimed to be very good at taxidermy, but when times were hard, he was able to supplement his wages with a case or two for a collector. He enjoyed "boxing up" the specimens which turned out well.

Ben Harwood, a shoemaker, student of the classics, and Primitive Methodist lay preacher, was, as Arthur described him "a sort of leather-stocking to three or four kindred souls who used to take short voyages with him into Broadland. Ben Harwood made a naturalist and Broadlander of me."

Taxidermy

The art of taxidermy began to decline after the First World War, as the craze for bird collections dwindled and once-valuable collections were broken up. However, in the 1870s, when Arthur was growing up, there was always a collector willing to pay for something out of the ordinary for his collection. In an obituary for Walter Lowne, a renowned Yarmouth taxidermist, Arthur wrote:

In the 1870s Walter Lowne and I were next-door neighbours. Having finished his apprenticeship as a carpenter at Martham, he came to live with an aunt. He had long been contemplating taking up taxidermy, and to that end he built a workshop in the little back garden. We talked birds over the fence.

I set him up with a book *"Gardner's Bird Stuffing"*. At that time we both carried 12-bores. His first experiment was on a starling. Then he obtained a cuckoo and commissioned "Juler", the taxidermist, to "set it up". He did.

Lowne carefully went through it, seeing how the wires were fastened, shape given to the body and so on, learning to stuff it - backwards. The poor starling was a weird bit of work!

Lowne took over Watson's noted game-dealer's shop, 40 Fuller's Hill, a stone's throw from St. Nicholas Church, Yarmouth. Its hooks had held thousands of pheasants, tens of thousands of rabbits and hares, wild geese, curlews, plovers, and others by the bunch. An otter was occasionally hung up for the public to gossip about, or a fox. As for wildfowl, Lowne took Arthur down to the cellar to look at the floorboards above head that were stained through with the blood of thousands.

Lowne was renowned for mounting his specimens in *"attitudes to resemble nature"*, and gained an award for his collection of birds at the Fisheries Exhibition in Great Yarmouth in 1881. The biggest challenge Lowne ever undertook was the preserving of the Lesser Rorqual Whale salvaged by the Gorleston lifeboatmen in 1891, and which Arthur "attended" as it travelled from place to place to go on public view. Lowne died in February 1915; he was 62. Arthur said:

He was buried in the quiet Belton Churchyard, a fitting corner for a man of his tastes, where the treecreepers flit from tree to tree, and the tits chatter their thin notes, and the chaffinch merrily calls to his mate on twig and tree branch in the hedgerow. Another link has been snapped between my olden days and the new

Of killing birds, Arthur wrote:

I had a gun more to assist study than kill and a gun was the means whereby I got out at three in the morning, or before day-light in all sorts of weather to get into bird land, year in and year out, after working long hours the day before.

Nowadays, a man or a boy can derive much joy from bird watching without the desire to kill. But he who uses his eyes gets more fun out of a country walk than he who goes over the ground as if he were racing for a wager. A naturalist may do much with his eyes, but books are a tremendous help. They are the signposts, which point a fellow to the correct road.

By 1891, Arthur had entirely discarded the gun as a "help" to observation, and derived comparably more real pleasure and interest in the pursuit of wild life with a field glass than he ever did with a fowling piece. He recalled:

I only regret that so many incidents in my books should relate to slaughter and sport. I believe I am a naturalist now, for I can admire nature without the slightest desire to destroy. All God's creatures seem to me now just like little friends, with whom I hold sweet converse, and whose society I enjoy. I like to write of them as if they were personal friends; surely if they thought me now as harmless as I am they would not shun my approaches as they do my fellows.

Arthur enjoyed the acquaintance of Mrs. E. Phillips, Vice-President of the Society for the Protection of Birds, and Hon. Sec. of the Croydon Branch. One of his earliest books, *"Man and Nature on the Broads"*, written in 1895, was dedicated to her. She appears to have been a big influence on him; even naming his youngest son, Gerald Phillips. He visited her once in London when she urged Arthur to drop caricatures and stick to bird drawings. To assist in the promotion of the protection of birds, he wrote a leaflet, No. 7, for the *Fur, Fin and Feather* series in May 1896. He was Honorary Secretary of the Great Yarmouth Section of the Norfolk and Norwich Naturalists' Society at the time, and a member complimented him by saying: *"It is writers such as you who do far more good than those not gifted with that charming style of expression. Girls will read yours when they will not look at a tract-like leaflet."* The leaflet was widely distributed, free, to anyone applying to Mrs. Phillips, and was said to have reached "Royal circles"! It was the fashion of the day for ladies to decorate their hats with feathers; specially favoured were plumes from breeding birds and this involved the mass slaughter of birds purely for the vanity of women.

A Protest by a Masculine Naturalist
"The Goura Mount"

I knew her when she was a girl, kind-hearted, gentle and good. She is all these now, but is a woman grown, with three pretty children prattling about the house, and enjoying all the comforts and delights which a happy marriage and easy means can give her. She never hurt a worm or killed a fly, once she nursed and tended a sparrow that some urchins had wounded with a catapult, and let it fly away on its recovery. She loves to ramble with her little ones beside her down a country lane, telling them how unkind it were to stone a chaffinch, entrap a linnet or shoot a sea gull. By precept and example, she teaches her children lessons of kindness to bird and beast and insect.

The other day I saw her at the milliner's. Trays upon trays and boxes upon boxes were spread upon the counter before her. An obliging damsel faced her; and the twin with dainty fingers handled spray after spray, and shook them to make each tuft display its loveliness. *Loveliness!* Alas! They were the spoils of some of the most beautiful of God's creatures. *She was buying ornamental hat-gear.* Her face beamed with satisfaction.

I stepped behind her, and told her the names of some of them, pointing out fragments of the plumage of the trogon, foreign kingfisher, mot-mots, parakeets and the whole and parts of humming birds. One tuft was made from seven different species - a wood owl, Impeyan pheasant, nightjar, Australian crested pigeon, bird of paradise, and two others. Australia, Asia, America and Europe had furnished victims for its concoction - a piece had been snatched from each and stitched together. "Five and two-three-farthings," said the damsel. "Here's a tuft much cheaper, one and a penny-farthing!" A turtle dove, a greenfinch and a lapwing had been sacrificed to make it. The kind-hearted woman-naturalist bit her lip, and calling the cheap article "common", laid it aside as fit only for some factory girl's fancy and purse.

"Aigrettes are becoming dearer, because scarcer," the young girl in black remarked.

"I'm sorry," said Madame, "and what are we to do when there are not more aigrettes? Use something else, I suppose. Flowers will then become more fashionable."

She was not sorry for the terrible waste of life and piteous scenes enacted in procuring these requirements of feminine vanity. Hers was only a selfish vexation. Over and over she turned the pile of lovely aigrettes. A thought crossed her mind that "they must indeed be beautiful creatures" which grew these feathers. Then her new Sunday hat flitted in front of them, and she only saw nature through her vanity and subservient to it.

"Here's a 'goura' mount," I heard the shop woman say; it will go well with the Chinchilla toque; price, complete, three guineas only."

"It is simply charming!" ejaculated my lady, springing with delight from off her chair, and sinking down again upon it. Then she clasped her hands and blessed herself, feeling at peace with Nature and all mankind.

I followed her out of the shop. A peevish boy was beating a donkey. My lady's heart yearned towards the ill-used ass. She crossed the muddy roadway and soundly rated the boy for his cruelty, calling a policeman's attention to it. A glow of satisfaction repaid her sacrifice of dainty boot and lady-like composure, for had she not performed a kindly action!

I saw her shortly after meeting a grim old fellow with two linnets cramped up in a six-inch prison. One bird was fluttering madly to find an outlet for escape. Its bill bore blood marks; it had chafed against the bars, which had cut across its forehead. In another cage, a puffed-out little thing, now past fluttering unrest - sat dumpy in the corner near the seed tray. Its head and wing coverts were ruffled. Tomorrow, that poor bird will want neither seed nor liberty. It will be dead and out of its misery.

I came up with Madame, as she turned her head away with a sigh. She said

A drawing of a lady wearing a Chinchilla toque, goura pigeon mount; price complete, £3 3s.   Chinchilla collarette, with real heads; £1 11s. 6d.

to me; "How wickedly cruel! Cannot such sufferings be prevented?"

I told her "No! - not while four pence was the saleable value of the little songsters - and there were folks to purchase."

Then I spoke out; I could not help it. As we walked along I told her of the gunners, whose special business it had been to exterminate the heronries, that *once* existed in Florida, by shooting the lovely white egrets as they flew to their nests in the tree tops. They had been to fish, and had brought their prey to give to the open-billed youngsters in the family nest. Danger was not apparent, perhaps, for the gunners lay hidden in their screens of brushwood and tangle. As the old birds dropped down to feed their young the cruel bullets killed them, some fell upon the earth in white lifeless heaps; some of their brood, and their life-blood stained their frightened little ones. Rudely the treetops were shaken, to fling the dead and living to the ground. Then, heedless of the cries and fluttering of the helpless nestlings, the iron heels of the bird-slaughterers might or might not crush them - if crushed, so much the better for them, for it ended their misery, and forewent starvation. Only the beautiful crests, dorsal plumes, and wing and tail coverts were wanted for the fair ladies in England. The mutilated carcases were left in heaps to rot and feed the blowflies. Many of the young died in their nests of sheer hunger. What mattered? Money was more than humanity, and gain than sentiment. Why did I speak in the past tense? Because I was obliged to, for such reckless slaughter has far more than decimated the race, and in many places the gunner has outlived his own unholy craft.

My lady coloured and bit her lip. She had not thus thought. I ventured to say a word on the cost of fur trimmings as well as of "Mixed Plumes", "Chinchillas are lovely animals. These pretty rodents once abounded in Chilli, Peru and Bolivia - up the rugged Andes - but their slaughter, paid for by those who can afford to wear the daintiest and rarest fur trimmings, was pushed with great ardour. Now their number is greatly diminished, thanks to English and other European ladies."

I told her of the *goura* pigeons; how that, ever-craving novelties, the dealer and the milliner sent their slaughterers yet farther and farther afield They have recently penetrated into New Guinea, and are slaying the noble Victoria crowned pigeon (*Goura Victoria*) for the sake of the top-knot on its head - to place it on a lady's! The goura is a pigeon large as a Chochin China fowl, the body of a slate-blue colour, with an eye of scarlet. These "parts" are valueless to the bird-hunter, and he leaves them to the rats and other vermin. Some specimens have bred in the Zoological Gardens, and on their first arrival were esteemed as noble creatures and as *rara aves.* "This pigeon," a writer stated in the 1860s "inhabits the southern parts of Northern Guinea, and is nowhere very numerous."

"So much the better!" replied the agents' employees. "We'll risk fevers and agues if you'll pay us well."

"Yes, yes!" said the ladies in purport, "get them by all means. We will not think of how they come to us. We like something that is beyond the reach of most women, from its scarcity and costliness, *and we are content to pay the price!"*

I saw a tear glisten in my friend's eye. The truth somehow had come home to her. I bade her "Good-day!"

Yesterday I met her, but without that chinchilla, goura-bedecked toque. Instead, I noticed a hat, becomingly arranged with dainty lace, knots of ribbon and wonderfully natural-looking flowers. I thought I never saw madame look so charming before. I heard a passer-by remark upon her beauty, and upon the distinction of her headgear; it was a lady who thus made comment, as might be expected, for it is their fashion.

Oh! That the women of England would pity the poor birds, and eschew feathers and crests and aigrettes. Surely art can furnish sufficient finery, without need of our robbing the tenants of our woods, of the forest and the mountainside, of their lives to steal from their lifeless carcases their beautiful attire. Oh! Pity them, for the sake of their helpless offspring that pine away, and starve, and die while the stench of their rotting parents pollutes the air and fills the nostrils of their perishing nestlings. I loathe a lady bedecked with feathers, and care not to bow in token of respect to her whose recognitions nods the plumes that disgrace her bonnet and her womanhood.

Chapter 7
BREYDON

"I used every opportunity to escape to the houseboat using the punt to get to and from it. Breydon grows on one so."

From the age of three Arthur Patterson had been taken by his father to his allotment garden at Runham Vauxhall. The gardens were separated from Breydon by a reedy ditch, the New Road, the railway, a wide marsh and the "walls" (embankments).

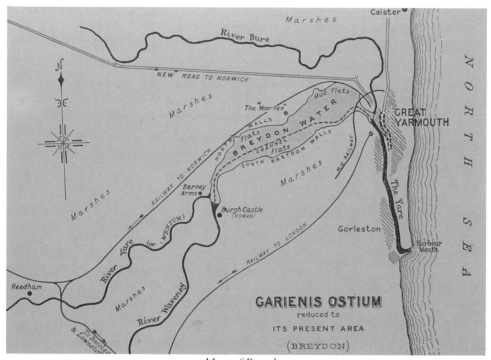

Map of Breydon

When I was sufficiently big to climb the tool shed, I used to do so to catch a glimpse of a silver streak that edged the apex of the walls at high water - *that was Breydon!* The boom of a distant punt-gun and the sharper crack of a fowling piece conjured up in my mind strange fancies, which were heightened by the scream of the startled wildfowl, and the passing to and fro overhead of great flocks of gulls.

I caught my first real glimpse of Breydon one day when, armed with a fish-head and a length of knotted twine, I slipped down, with other muddy urchins, unknown to my father, to the riverside, in quest of a "sea-sammy" (crab), which I dared not take home. My father's inveterate abhorrence of the "muddy, dangerous place", only served to increase my interest in it, and as I

38

became still keener to explore it, I would skulk at the heels of any tolerant gunner to get on to the "walls", or ramble to its vicinity whenever opportunity offered. I shall never forget my first sail across Breydon in Ben Harwood's punt and whose boat-shed adjoins my own today. Since those days of dreaming I have spent many pleasant hours upon and around this favourite haunt, in companionship with the birds that frequent it, and the rugged men who, from hard necessity as well as instinctive liking, have tried to make a precarious living out of its oozy depths.

"Breydoners"

The county of Norfolk has always been noted for its lovers of natural history, its ornithologists in particular, thanks to its outstanding and fortunate position "on the map", where breckland, broad and mudflat, marsh and sea-beach combined to attract numbers of birds and an easy access into their favourite haunts. Observation on our spring and autumnal migrations has always been an alluring hobby and has added a great deal to our literature; but a certain class that included the educated, richer vandal have for many decades pursued - raged unholy war, in fact, upon our avian population. The extermination of our Ruffs and Reeves, as Broadland nesting birds, was greatly due to the ardour of collectors, helped by the rapacity of dealers in coveted eggs and most wicked of the barbarians were those who remorselessly exterminated the Norfolk race of Great Bustards, and those meaner fellows who nearly accomplished the clearance of the Bearded Tit. As far back as the writings of Moses suggestion has been made touching Man's right to kill.

I have been astonished at the impunity with which my old Breydon men would risk extremes of temperature. If you had entered one of these eelmen-wildfowlers' tarry houseboats, in the 1860s and 70s, you would have discovered therein a temperature of over 100 degrees; thick with tobacco smoke. There sat the old fellow roasting, awaiting the coming of fowl, or the lifting of the tide - to turn out with scarcely an additional rag on their backs - into the stinging wind, cold below freezing point.

To my mind there is not another nature book dealing with the Fauna of Norfolk that compares with the Rev. Richard Lubbock's *"Observations on the Fauna of Norfolk"*, which deals more particularly on the District of the Broads. Lubbock was born in 1798, took his B.A. degree in 1824 and that of M.A. in the ensuing year; he was ordained in the following year. He had lived in the same parish thirty-nine years as rector of Eccles, Norfolk; and in writing his inimitable Fauna - his one small book, which has in its second edition two biographical chapters written by the late Sir Thomas Southwell and Henry Stevenson, both excellent Norwich naturalists.

Always favouring the protection of our native birds and using many endeavours on their behalf, it was not until about the year 1867 that Mr. Morris commenced that determined and systematic agitation for his friends in feather, which was carried on for so many years. This labour of love would have been deemed a life's work for some. His suggestion for a tax on guns was practically the opening of his campaign. The late Rev. Francis Orper Morris began his campaign for Protection of Birds in October 1869; before and after that date he had waged warfare against the wanton destruction of our sea and land-birds.

The Act for the Preservation of Some Birds (seabirds) came in in 1869. Further protection for other birds came in 1872, with another act in 1876. These were all repealed in 1880 with the Wild Birds Protection Act, which for the first time, prescribed a close season for all birds, to run from 1st March to 31st July.

In 1880 the Breydon Wild Birds' Protection Society employed a watcher to make daily observations of the wild birds that frequented the famous stretch of water on the borders of Yarmouth. "Ducker" Chambers was appointed the First Watcher. He met with a very hostile reception, because the Close Season was to affect Breydon, and the crowd that then carried guns afloat, or on shore. Not that he cared, for he had been a noted boxer, of big bodily build, he was bluff and a little boisterous, and not by any means officious. Breydon was yet harbouring various birds in their season, among them occasionally spoonbills and avocets, and perchance among the crowds of small wading birds, birds of exceptional value from a bird collector's point of view, when "Ducker" was chosen by a committee to see that gunning ceased for the season. But just think what a task it was to police the whole area of many hundred acres of mudflats and crinkling drains.

In the 70s and 80s when I was frequently afloat, birds were more abundant, on migration, and there were collectors always ready for bargains; two or three subtle sportsmen who did not depend on shooting, played an occasional trick on Ducker. After a night at home they would way-lay him and cajole him into the Cobholm Tavern or another hotel of a kind and discuss various bird matters in common. *"Would he - could he do with a pint?"* Could he not? He was a very droughty old fellow. Pot after pot vanished until Ducker went off into a drowsy, irresistible snoring state and in the meantime Albert Beckett, "Pero" Pestell, and "Pintail" Thomas had rowed hurriedly upstream. In an hour or so Ducker was rowing round the "Captives", but one and another had reached the Breydon North Wall and put the old man ashore, and in a bag or basket at once crossed the marshes, and made for the "Bowling Green Pub", where they would effect a remunerative sale from rival stuffers and collectors. If our local gunners found themselves outwitted, they would leave one in the boat, whilst another clambered up the walls, and stalked off to some haystack and with care hid the bird in it to be called for later on. Godwits in the red, and knots, black-breasted plovers, an avocet and another desirable bird or two had seen the last of Breydon, and lands beyond the sea. Bird-folks who were egg collectors, dealers in birds and eggs and collectors, were always on the alert and were not unlike competitive "bookies" at the racecourse that did their best to outwit anybody else. It so happened that Beckett was first "victim" and was a splendid, and a humorous transgressor. Chambers for 11 years roughly and intermittently kept a notebook. He died in the Fishermen's Hospital, and featured in *"Nature in Eastern Norfolk"*.

In the summer of 1889, the Bird Protection Society was founded; its first president, was Winifred, Duchess of Portland. It was formerly called the Fur, Fin and Feather Society. The Society was incorporated under Royal Charter in 1904. During the First World War there was a resting of the breeding grounds. Today the Royal Society for the Protection of Birds is Europe's largest and most forward-looking conservation organisation, with over one million members.

Chapter 8
GEORGE JARY – BREYDON BIRD WATCHER

"These humble Breydon men have always appealed to me."

The Watcher's Boat

In the spring of 1900, George Jary was appointed Watcher - nicknamed "Newcome" he was met with a warm reception - jeers and insults, which he took in good part, and for a number of years to 1926 he faithfully served his employers. Arthur wrote of Jary as being one of his best chums; and with whom he jogged along for forty-odd years without a grumble or an unkind word. During the summer of 1921 Arthur spent a two-week holiday on Jary's houseboat on Breydon and wrote a series of articles for the Norwich Mercury series called *Holiday Nights and Days on Breydon.* In one of them he described the houseboat.

The hull of the houseboat, nicknamed "The Pickletub", had been a fishing smack's ferryboat, a species of vessel that got many a hard knock when ferrying fish upon the North Sea. The houseboat lay moored in a cross-drain running at right angles to the Ship drain, immediately opposite the few weed-clothed timbers of the good ship Agnes.

The Pickletub as a houseboat ought to be at least leak-proof, but old age brings on infirmities, aggravating them with the passing of time. *"I usually take out three or four large buckets of water the last thing at night,"* said Jary; sounding the well next morning with a little degree of interest. A trifle of water left in a houseboat is said, by aquatic experts, "to sweeten" it. I'd rather it remained a trifle sour!

Some uncanny sort of red paint is fading on Jary's outside walls; the cabin-top is tarred black and dull as the curate's hat the stableman now wears; and the hull festooned with fenders, unbeautiful, but necessary as a caution to the restless punts on either side, is weatherworn and hungry for a dab or two of tar. Inside, the 9-foot cabin is "settled" on either side, with a convenient cupboard in every corner. A small *"Dee"* yacht's stove is adorned with a couple of brick-built hobs, whitewashed, and a cast-iron pipe pokes up through the roof, to deliver the smoke of it to the four winds of Heaven, which ever wind chooses to reject it. As I scribble, a teapot is concocting "dye" for Jary on the hob; a fry pan of goodly circumference hangs from a nail behind the chimney, like a soiled banjo. Turn it round, and no scullery maid could show a cleaner one; and alongside it is a gridiron manufactured by the captain himself that suggests a zither. It hath made many a bloater tune up to it. Three of the cupboards contain Jary's crockery, oddments, and comestibles, respectively; in the fourth, yours truly has stowed away bread, sugar, tea, and other creature comforts, Friar's balsam, soda, and other remedial devices, as well as specimen bottles which are getting well tenanted.

A small clock ticks furiously on the tiny mantelshelf, where pipes - more or less burnt up - and matches bear it company. A looking glass that rejects one's face, or else distorts it, hath upon it an age-worn, sickly smile, like dirty pewter, and hangs above the clock. Beside it hangs the spring balance that, in its time, hath weighted the fate of tons of eels, which in these latter degenerate days is inscribed; "Mene, mene, tekel, upharsin," the emphasis being on the "tekel!" One or two little bird pictures hang upon the walls.

My bedding is on the starboard settle; Jary's is all to port. My small pickling mattress is filled with comfortable oat-straw, inside which a few refractory straws have once in a while to be mollified by a shaking. Two big warm army blankets make a fellow snug and cosy. For the bolster, there is the kit bag containing an aged coat or two - old age pensioners - that can take no harm or hurt. My second kit bag holds a few oddments of unspoilable apparel, and reinforces my bolster; the little green velveteen pillow that solaced my Broadland nights does so today, to speak a trifle incorrectly. My faithful glasses on which so much depends are ever at my elbow. One other item: I have made a rough book-case yesterday out of a margarine box; on its shelves are two beloved volumes of Thoreau's *"Concord"* and *"Walden"*, a little book or two of marine-things, one also of my own - *"Nature in Eastern Norfolk"*, and a bundle of half-used copy-books for writing. An eel-pick, a butt-dart, and a net are at hand, and Jary's tin of worms hath leave to dwell in a special corner; for are they not almost as rare as dodos in these hot, dry days?

On the first day of his holiday, August 5th,1921 Arthur rowed his punt out and fastened it to the Pickletub.   Jary prophesied a blow; he said he "*didn't like the look of things",* and went home for the night. Arthur meant to stick it out in the houseboat. The night came on, a wild, weird night; overhead was blackest darkness, save to the right, where the lights of Norwich glared on the sky afar off; a sign, my skipper had warranted me, that meant a *stiffish* blow: he had seen it *aforetime*. The water gleamed phosphorescently as it rippled over the mooring ropes, and parted round the punt and smelt-boat's stems. When the cabin door was shut the wind hummed ominously among the poles on the cabin top, coarsening into the wail of the sea-wolf. It was eerie and made one's nerves tense; one, wondered whether another Lodbrog (the Viking) would be adrift before morning, to land on Burgh flats, or at Reedham. Jary had had a rough night in June, when three stakes of his four were drawn and the boat helplessly bumped her keel upon the adjoining flat, her only mooring being strained to the utmost, until the tide fell, leaving him stranded. His boat had rolled until the sills of the cabin windows were very nearly licked worse on next morning's tide: I managed, however, to snatch a sleep when the night tide had gone down …

A little before midnight there broke out a startling hubbub among the greater black-backed gulls, which had been washed off the flat by the tide's highest effort. They were a-wing; and their noisy "Yah-oh! O-lawk! O-lawk! O-lawk!" made one think of troubled spirits and drowned seafarers… Had I been asleep, and dreaming, or what? Did my eyes play me false? For, on turning, I was made aware of other Voices, as of the Night: and there appeared to my astonished senses a quartet of uninvited, unexpected intruders, who had probably run in from the Vasty Darkness, belated. Their presence seemed real to me, but of me they took not the slightest notice. I did not hear their incoming, nor did I feel any inclination to resent it.

On the opposite settle, where Jary always sleeps, sat three old fellows with whom I have often hobnobbed and somewhat written of. The boat now floated on an even keel, for all the Presences of the Four Immortals. "Pintail" Thomas had in his crippled hand a dead dunlin; in its day it had gathered many a hundred - even ten score after a shot. He sat there, with his "cripple-stopper" across his knee, as I have him camera-depicted at home, on the wall.

Pintail Thomas

Breydon's done for," said Pintail Thomas, *"for us old gunners; the drained meshes (marshes); the blank trains runnin' all round it; the close season, and them grow'd up flats; fare no use tryin' to get a boat round even at high water, on the nape-tides; lor' in the 1870s you could still git a livin'.*

"A pipe of 'bacca for brekfist, and tew for tea!" retorted the quick-tempered Thomas. *"Theer ain't no collectors, nowadays, to buy rare 'uns; and fowl don't fare wanted by people now furrign meat is cheap. Lost taste for 'em, tew. Besides, with them decoys, there ain't none! The rich urns fare to get all!"*

Breydoner (possibly Short-un Page) going eel-fishing

A Breydoner "picking" for eels

Little "Short'un Page", whose big boots, like the sea boots of Thomas, totalled half the height of either men, neither of them five-footers, promptly dried up as the gunner snapped out his words. Poor little Short'un sat there next him moodily cogitating, his quaint gold earrings vibrating to the movements of the boat, his ringlets falling around his neck, his head nodding in the pert old sparrow-like way. *"Smeltin', let alone eel-catchin', was done, tew!"*

"Tea," said Snicker Larn, of the Roman Profile: *"smelts ain't what they wor; and them River Preservers done us, when we could get a few scoor on a tide. The only place wheer smelters get a livin' is in the Workhus."*

Snicker and Short'un were co-workers in that hard life of Breydon. Born to it, their last days were spent in the neighbourhood of their beloved Breydon; the Old Age Pension just saved them from the "Workhus." The fourth Presence, I must call "The Unknown"; he was an old-time gunner of the 40s, who had shot up here when the others were small boys, before Fielding and "Punt" Palmer and Squire Berney were of the cult of the "gentlemen gunners", whose henchmen, "Silky" Watson, "Pero" Pestell, "Pintail", "Baker Stork", Thacker, and others, were. "The Unknown's" attire was of the Early Victorian style: his gun was flintlock, the picture of neatness and finish; a shoulder strap held his horn of powder and another slung crosswise, his flask of shot. Their punts lay moored outside on the darksome waters.

All their talk was of matters of Breydonian interest, or vanished fowl, of departed kindred spirits, now in the Happy Hunting-grounds, of things that were, and are, and will not be full soon.

"Pintail" drew Jary's poker from the fire, and with it lit his pipe, handing it to "Short-un" who did the same, and to "Snicker," who also lighted up; and in meditative manner they filled the cabin with tobacco smoke, which made a haziness that vastly added to the weirdness of this midnight hour. The silence, that comes over men whose idol is the narcotic weed, affected them, and made one's feelings tense and strangely queer.

"The Unknown" held his hand up negatively, and with authoritative gesture, and in a faraway sort of voice, offered to recite a bit of verse, which my mind so gripped that I append it. He thus began:

A Breydoner's Lament
(To assist the reader with local names, a glossary of bird-names is given in brackets. It is probable that Arthur was the author).

Cum list to me, ye Breydoners
While I tell in lines o' rhyme
Of our doin's in the old days
What have fled on wings o' time.
When the old flats swarmed with wildfowl
When the godwicks came in clouds; (godwits)
And the pipin' full-eyed plovers (grey plovers)
Roamed the ooze in feedin' crowds.

When the black terns tript like swallows
As they made for Upton lake,
When the fish-hawks in the channel (ospreys)
Dove for butts from many a stake;
While the knots and stints and dottrel (stint = dunlins, dottrell=ringed plovers)
Came in bunches thousands strong;
Keepin' well in front of weather
What the north wind driv' along.

When the brent and saw-bill follered (brent = brent goose, saw-bill = goosander, merganser)
With the tufty, teal and nun; (tufty = tufted duck, nun = smew)
When we fowlers got among 'em
With the deadly old flint gun.
And the outlook fared like Grinland,
And thuck ice froze round the stakes,
And the hard-fowl drop't in hundreds (diving ducks)
In the broken watery wakes.

When the wild swans flew in wedges
And fat geese was wondrous tame,

When slick loons dove like the litenin' (loons = divers)
And shy pokers done the same. (pochards)
Them were days in which we revelled
When we risk'd the ice and squalls
Days when we could make a livin'
Both afloat and round the walls.

But we better like the May-birds
In theer new spring plumage drest;
When in luck we got the spune-bills, (spoonbills)
Cobble-bills and all the rest, (avocets)
When the cock smee whistles "smee-on" (wigeon)
And he dabbled to his mate;
When he draw'd the long duck-grass up,
For the sweet roots what they ate.

When the gay old mallards joined 'em
For the dibble up the ponds;
While the fludd-tide driv' the curlews
For a gossip on the ronds;
But the glory's gone for ever,
Our old pals lie in the dust
And the fowl have with 'em vanished
And the ducks gone to rust.

A tense silence again fell upon the strange gathering; and one by one the old fellows from the spirit world rose and filed out of the Pickletub, and dropping into their shadowy, worn punts, huskily bade good night, and vanished in the gloom, not plying their oars, as I expected, for there, outside, had awaited them, the rude and squalid old Charon, with bushy, grey beard, and feeble eyes, and ragged uniform; his fare a halfpenny, to such as these, although he could demand three. He had the ghosts speedily in tow, and vanished with them down the Styx, and over the waters of Acheron. I rubbed my eyes; but they were gone. Had I been dreaming?

When George Jary, the Bird-watcher, died in December 1934, Arthur wrote these words about him to the *Eastern Daily Press*.

The remains of George Jary, after many years of faithful service as bird watcher on Breydon, will be laid to rest today. A long illness, a legacy of stormy nights and days, preceded his death, which took place in the week, at the age of 75, and there are very few of his old associates of the punt-gun and smelt-net, to mourn his loss. He was generally liked, notwithstanding the antipathy which followed the edicts for the protection of birds. It was a hard life out there, sleeping in a hut built on an old "hull" described as a houseboat; in all weathers - in early spring snows and hailstorms whitened the tarred roof and heavy gales tossed the craft as she lay moored in mid-Breydon, as near to a sheltering patch of mud-flat as possible.

Jary was altogether more alert than the first watcher, "Ducker" Chambers, and the sly visits of the more daring defiers of the law ceased. Now and then a pot-shot from the gun of some stupid or ignorant summer yachtsman broke the peace, and brought Jary to "see to it", but adverse winds and bared mudflats made pursuit usually abortive. Still, he, like sturdy old "Ducker" Chambers, got a case once in a while. Ducker was slow and fearless; he had in his earlier years "fought in the ring" with honours. He occasionally stepped ashore; the fraternity quickly knew of it, and were out and afloat by day dawn, and got home their game, which were spoonbills, and other desirable waders, for at that time stuffed birds brought in money.

Jary netted very good soles before pollution had so spoiled the waters. Flounders and many interesting fishes came into the net. Eels were speared; and there were frequently remunerative catches in the smelt-nets. Later he made a living by his draw-net. For many years he presented his annual notebook to the society's secretary. He had on two or three occasions fallen overboard. He could not swim; so he rolled over, and floated on the tide until some observer came to help him. Jary was not a great talker, and was no storyteller, but he once gave me an account of a dog that stole and ate live eels out of his bucket. He told the publican that, after he had wakened up to the loss, he noticed a dog whose body was remarkably distended; it stood out like a balloon. *"Never mind,"* said Boniface, *"I'll get you some more,"* and he hauled out half a stone from the lock and satisfied Jary. It always tickled poor Jary whenever I started the story.

Jary's deafness had greatly spoiled his later life; and he developed into insanity. I have written a great deal about him in my various books.

The Watcher, George "Newcome" Jary in his punt in 1927

The Watcher's Notes on the Birds protected on Breydon, for the 1912 season.

5 March	About 80 wigeon, some curlews and a great flock of knot
6 March	About 100 wigeon, and couple of geese here
10 March	About 120 wigeon, some curlew, knot, and hundreds of dunlin and ring plover
13 March	About 200 wigeon, some curlew, and thousands of dunlin and ring plover, and knot here this evening
14 March	First heard the summer call of the redshank this evening, and afterwards saw a little flock
22 March	Nearly 300 wigeon here today, and a great number of small birds
28 March	About the same quantity of wigeon, and some pintail, a couple of geese and several old herons here
31 March	The wigeon are nearly all gone, and two geese are still here, also several curlew, and a great many dunlin and ring plover
6 April	The two geese are still here with several old herons and curlew, but the wigeon are nearly all gone now
11 April	Some shovelers, pintail and a couple of shelduck, and great flocks of dunlin and ring plover, and a few redshank
13 April	A blacktail godwit here this evening
17 April	A few grey plover and some godwit here this morning, great numbers of dunlin and ring plover, some redshank, and two geese
21 April	More godwit and a few whimbrel here this morning
22 April	Saw a swallow for the first time this morning
25 April	A good many birds here now; a lot more whimbrel and godwit, some in their summer plumage, some knot with about two thousand ring plover and dunlin
2 May	Two spoonbills here this morning, also some greenshank
4 May	The spoonbills are still here this morning, also a few common tern
6 May	Another spoonbill came and joined the other two this morning
7 May	The three spoonbills are still here this morning, also some shelduck and a lot of whimbrel and godwit, and numbers of dunlin and some grey plover
9 May	The spoonbills and some lesser tern
11 May	The spoonbills are gone today
13 May	Scores of whimbrel here now all over the place, several godwit, some lesser tern, and hundreds of dunlin and ring plover
14 May	A black tern here today
16 May	Several turnstones, godwit and lesser tern
20 May	Another spoonbill here this morning, a very good old bird
22 May	Another spoonbill here this morning, there are two here now
23 May	The spoonbills are still here, but the whimbrel and godwit are all gone now
25 May	The spoonbills are still here, also several lesser tern and some turnstones

27 May	Spoonbills left this morning about 9 o'clock
28 May	Three black tern here today and some lesser tern
2 June	Some red knot, lesser tern and black-breasted grey plover, and several ring plover
4 June	Three tame swans here this morning
5 June	Three spoonbills here this morning
8 June	Three spoonbills are still here today, also some shovelers and lesser tern, knot, dunlin and ring plover
9 June	Spoonbills gone today
10 June	Nine shovelers, some knot and a good many redshank, some dunlin and ring plover
15 June	Four shelduck and some lesser tern
17 June	A cormorant here today
19 June	A whimbrel and several curlew
25 June	Some shelduck and scores of old and young redshank
2 July	Some young mallard, a lot of old and young herons, redshank, dunlin, and ring plover,
3 July	Some common tern
7 July	A flock of about 20 shelduck
8 July	Several birds beginning to come now, some whimbrel, very many redshank, some dunlin and ring plover and young herons
12 July	A young loon here today, also a good many other birds, several whimbrel and a nice flock of knot, some mallard
13 July	A spoonbill here this morning, quite a young bird
16 July	Spoonbill still here today, also a lot of whimbrel, redshank, several young mallard and shovelers
19 July	Another spoonbill here this morning, so there are two here now, also a lot of whimbrel and hundreds of redshank
21 July	Spoonbills are gone today
23 July	The spoonbills are back again today
26 July	The spoonbills are gone today
27 July	A good flock of lesser tern and some common tern
29 July	A little flock of teal, some mallard, and a lot of lesser tern and some common tern
29 July	A little flock of teal, some mallard, and a lot of lesser tern here this evening
3 August	Some turnstones here today, also a good many lesser tern
5 August	A lot of lesser tern, scores of whimbrel, curlew, dunlin, and ring plover
6 August	A spotted redshank here today
7 August	A very good black tern here today, also scores of lesser tern, common tern, and some sandwich tern, which were flying very high to the southeast tonight.
11 August	There are a lot of birds here.

Arthur at William Durrant's Game Stall on Yarmouth
Market where the Breydoners traded their wildfowl

Chapter 9
SOME OLD YARMOUTH SPORTSMEN

"Today the men and their vocations have vanished."

During the War, in a letter to a friend, Arthur wrote:

October 11th, 1915
Dear Sir
Bor', how yew dew tork! To be shure! Why I'm alive an' kickin' as usurel, just as yew fare to be doin' of.
Yes I still go watching the birds at leisure time: and running after the kiddies at others (here he refers to his work as School Attendance Officer).

Mutual surprise on the Breydon Walls

I expect you see the *Mercury* and old Melinda Twaddles Notions. The cartoons are all right for the time of the War. So you see the War affects everyone more or less.
I still follow up old Breydon - my first Houseboat is now shored up on the bank as you see it in *"Wild Life on a Norfolk Estuary"* but I sold it to Blyth in the Electric Works here, for a shooting box. I've got a small boat in a creek

up the Duffells Rond; and a double cabin boat on the river. The latter has a lavatory in the bows so you see I am quite civilised, even with my trousers down! When I can sit and grunt and watch birds to my heart's content! Old Jimmy Hurr is still alive, 80 - or thereabouts. Dye is blind you know, but I occasionally take him for a row. Hurr sits and reads the *Daily News* to him in the bake office. Lowne is dead; all the old Breydoners too, Lucky Bob died a week or two ago. Snicker Larn is dead, - only Shortun Page survives among the smelters, and Fred Clarke, the gunners. I fancy old Gibbs the puntgunner is alive, but feeble, and lives at Gorleston.

I've got a book on the go - I may finish the manuscript this winter, - can't say, as the War spoils one for writing - "The Snipe Shooters' Club", a rollicking story of old Breydoners.

Yours, AHP

Arthur wrote much about his acquaintance with the men, who made their scant living from Breydon by shooting and poaching, *Wildfowlers and Poachers* being his greatest testament to them, which was published in 1929. In 1934, the year before Arthur died, he wrote a series for the *"Yarmouth Mercury"* under the title *"Some Old Breydon Sportsmen,* and appealed for photographs; many were sent in. He said:

By bringing these chapters dealing with Breydon men, both rich and poor, to a close, it seems like bidding a second good-bye to a lot of old friends, whose survivors may be counted on one's fingers today.

Arthur "mardling" with an old sailor.

Arthur at a Yarmouth boatyard

The great age to which the Breydoners lived speaks well for the salubrity of Breydon muds and waters. By 1934, with the exception of two or three, all the rest have passed into the Great Beyond. Fred Clarke 84, Jack Gibbs 88, "Strike" Sharman 86, Ben Harwood 81, Charlie Harwood 81, "Old Sharper" 86, "Billy Sharper" 84, George Blake 81, Arthur Brand 77, "Old Bessey" 82, "Fiddler" Gordens 82, Ben Dye 77, "Mr" Dugdale 76, Jack Quinton 81, and there were other notables including "Jimmy" Hurr, "Patty" Westgate, "Limpenny" King, "Saltfish" Jex, "Admiral" Gooch, "Trotter" Lodge, "Old Stork" Thacker, and "Little Billy" Thacker, his brother "Billy" Thacker.

Some of the Breydoners ended their days in the Fishermen's Hospital: "Pintail" Thomas, who died in 1901; another was the first (bird) watcher, Ducker Chambers. The "Hospital", a collection of fourteen cottages each with the privacy of its own front door, provided homes for fisherman over the age of 60; if married, their wives accompanied them.

The Fishermen's Hospital, off Yarmouth market place.
Reproduced from P H Emerson's "Wild Life on a Tidal Water"

Much was written about "Pintail" Thomas in Arthur's various books ("Pintail" appeared in the imaginary scene aboard Jary's houseboat in 1921, with "Snicker" Larn and "Short-un" Page). Of these latter two, Arthur wrote:

Snicker" could not be cajoled into church. *"Look, ere,"* said he, *"I can't come to goin' in there; it look to me as if I was hangin'around after suffin'. I can't do it!"* Larn was a lovable old fellow. He was humoured, for he was fond of advising his chums who had pains and aches. He eloquently praised his patents for quack nostrums that *"would cure all your scrumatic",* and other portents as well, if they trusted to Snicker, who posed as a semi-physician! He died around the turn of the century.

Arthur attended most of the funerals of the Breydoners, but unavoidably missed that of "Short-un" Page. On seeing Arthur Patterson, "Stork" Thacker said:

"We didn't see you when little old Short-un was put under the daisies yesterday. I s'pose you was too busy. Well, it was a rummin'. We berried him in his poor brother Stevey's grave what was built for two. And just as we was low'rin' him inter the syle, theer cum up a voice, solumn and slow - it was his brother's voice, an' it says 'Hallo, boy Short'un, here you be then, But hev yew brung any bacca long with yer?' "

Just as I did 50 years ago, I did today (Boxing Day 1929) - took a lonely ramble. First I visited my first angler friend, poor old wooden-legged Sharman. In a little two-roomed cottage he sat beside a small fire; at 88 worn out, and dispirited. He was sorting out English stamps and others into envelopes for a son who does a little dealing with boys in stamps. His old merry self had settled into a despondent ancient: I could not get a joke - as of old - responded to. His daughter works about 12 hours a day and sees after him the rest. His eyesight seems as good as my own. Just imagine a good moral old chap whiling away his time to the grave - never seeing the outside sunshine! I might add here that Sharman and I for many years amused a great crowd of infants every Sunday afternoon at the Primitive Methodist Temple - rarely less than 80 of them, who revelled in my blackboard talks, and the old harmonium's output. Thence I rounded up another 80- odder whose whole life is a grumble. He took me upstairs to see the water percolating through the ceiling, and damned the landlord - who perhaps deserves it. This old chap otherwise is ever optimistic, always going to do great things.

Arthur on a lonely ramble

Chapter 10
SCHOOL ATTENDANCE OFFICER

"I was never happier than as School Attendance Officer. I have refused more promising offers because I am satisfied with my present work, and nature in Broadland has stronger attractions for me than anywhere else."

Arthur at his desk in the School Board Offices

Arthur Patterson commenced his duties as a School Attendance Officer in Southtown, Great Yarmouth, in 1892. At the time the town swarmed with truants and irregulars, school attendances were low, and officers were often greeted by offensive names. At the end of his 20 years' Attendance Officership he was called "Mr." and treated with respect. His efforts, it is said, enabled the Truant School at Southtown to be closed.

An article was written about him in *The School Attendance Gazette* in June 1902, in which it was said:

One of the most prominent characters in the town of Great Yarmouth is Mr. Arthur Patterson, who by his skill as a naturalist, a writer and cartoonist, has won for himself a unique position. His remarkable ability in this work is only equalled by his success as a school attendance officer, a work for which he appears to be especially fitted and which he has carried on for a number of years, to the entire satisfaction of the School Board and the teachers in his district. In carrying out his duties, he shows remarkable tact, and frequently by diplomacy and good-natured banter, accomplishes that which the arm of the law had failed to do. That he has the best interests of the children at heart goes without saying, and whether it is getting a ticket for clothing or for the hospital, obtaining a situation for a lad, or drawing a grotesque figure for the amusement of a sick child, he does it all with a good humour, and parents begin to see that he is a friend and not an enemy, as many had supposed. While kindness is his ruling principle, yet he combines with it great firmness, and not a single delinquent escapes his notice. Armed with a walking stick with a large crook, he may be seen at all important weddings, funerals, processions, and other frolics, and woe to the absconding one who comes within reach of that crook. He is quickly hooked out of the crowd, and his name and address taken for future reference. Many anecdotes might be told of A.P. and his work, but one or two must suffice.

The Fishwharf, a haven for truants, where boys begged herrings, and their parents encouraged them

On one occasion he visited the Fishwharf during the fishing season, and there found a gang of truants with a quantity of stolen herrings in a barrow, which they had borrowed, intending to hawk the fish in the town. When A.P. arrived, the boys decamped, leaving our friend in the awkward possession of a barrow of stolen fish. At another time he discovered some truants in a yard surrounded by a wooden fence which he attempted to scale, but in his anxiety to reach the culprits failed to notice the tenter-hooks with which the *fence was covered until he found himself suspended in mid-air by the nethermost part of his trousers, much to the amusement of the boys, who, it is needless to say, met their deserts later on.*

A.P. has a keen sense of the humorous side of life, and contrives to get much amusement out of the variety of cases with which he has to deal; so much so that not infrequently the magistrates are keenly amused at his ready answers and quaint witticisms, while his remarks at the Attendance Committee meetings cause much amusement. An amusing case came under the writer's notice, in which a boy's grandmother appeared to give reason for his non-attendance. The old lady was very deaf, and all attempts to make her hear appeared fruitless until A.P. appeared on the scene. Hastily taking in the situation, he procured a sheet of brown paper out of which he improvised a trumpet, and putting the small paper end into the old lady's ear he proceeded to investigate the case, the old girl declaring she "could hear bootiful."

In a letter in 1915 Arthur made the following note and illustration:

Mr. Patt'son after a truant

I looked round a corner of the Fishwharf today and the one truant, spotting me, fled, leaving a putrid mackerel in his flight! What a terror I must be!

I am sure there are very few who write, who sit down at night as I do exhausted in body and worried by a day's hard visiting. I often make as many as ninety calls on erring parents in a day. Last night I sat down fagged and with a blistered foot and under-linen damp with the perspiration of the day. I have frequently sat down to scribble and had to desist after a few lines and tumble into my bed, my brains absolutely refusing to assist my fingers.

I have been, somewhere, thought to be brutal. I deny that. I never caned a boy in anger; nor told him that it hurt me as much as it did him. A real boy hates a lie, even as a compliment. Every "bad" boy has a sporting chance; it was generally his two young legs against my older. If he won the race, I lost; and vice versa and both accepted the position truthfully. I could count the number of "twicers" on less than my two hands; the third dose was taken by less than the digits of my left hand.

I spotted a troublesome boy, bolting. I knew him and went to the house; and the fond mother came out to excuse him. He had gone upstairs and was busy directly over the windowsill - the rascal emptied a flowerpot of dry mould over my head!

Mothers are a study in themselves; and one is apt to learn to speedily "read" character.

"Do you think that answer is a lie?" once asked a woman.

"My Good Woman," I said, *"I haven't suggested such a thing."*

"No, but you looked it in your eye!"

I looked again and assured her, *"It's all right madam, I am quite satisfied with your answer."*

The vast majority of children are naturally truthful and it is abominable for anyone without just cause to accuse a child of stealing or lying. A child's nature is peculiarly sensitive and a wrong rankles long. Fifty-six years ago, I was watching mackerel being ferried ashore on Yarmouth Beach and like most boys I thought a fresh fat mackerel a rare prize, if come by honestly.

"Master," I said to the fisherman, *"give us a mackerel,"* and the man handed me one. I went home with it delighted. My stepmother was a Puritan in her way; and she accused me of stealing it. No protest from me was accepted. She threw the fish in the street. To be branded a liar deeply cut me; I had rather been whipped. The memory and the mental picture of that episode remain vivid to this day. So I always start with a boy without questioning his honour, troublesome as he may be: I do not call him a sinner for truanting but we both understand it is a breach of etiquette, a sort of bad slip that may lead to untoward incidents, and reprisals.

When walking through George Street with a friend one Sunday noon, I espied seven sturdy lads chatting and playing on the pavement near a little Mission Hall. I did not know them but they knew me.

"Take no notice," I hinted to my friend, *"If these lads cut up a bit rough and rude, they mean no harm."*

As we came up to them, the ringleader said, *"Fall in"*, *"Shun"* and they did it smartly, and in the next crisp order he said: *"Sal –ute"*, which he and the others did prettily; accompanying the action with - *"Good Old Patterson!"*

I tell you that little bit of boy-nature touched one to the quick! I knew that they meant it.

It is often a pleasure to me nowadays to be stopped by grown men, often strangers to me, who thanked me for the pains I took - and the pains I gave.

Not seldom do little chaps pull my coat-tails in the street and say *"Mr. Pepmint! I go to 'cole now!"*

"Court Martial" - an every day incident
One of the cartoons from a souvenir commemorating Arthur's
Twenty Years' Work as an Attendance Officer, dated November 1912

This cartoon was one of several published in a souvenir by Arthur to mark the end of 20 years' Attendance Officership. He said:

My work has been congenial, and has not lacked variety. I have endeavoured to do my best; and have, I hope, done my share towards the betterment of our poorer children. In my experience there has been much pathos that touches, and not a little humour that tickles. In 1892, an Attendance Officer was often greeted by names not so inoffensive or dignified as his own; today he is a "Mr." and is respectfully treated, whilst boys salute him with hands that are empty – if grimy.

Most respectfully do I record my appreciation of my Committee, who have never doubted my honesty, or sought to impose any task that jarred upon my conscientious scruples. I would also mention the general good feeling and helpfulness existing between the Office Staff, my Head Teachers, and myself."

Chapter 11
THE GORLESTON WHALE

"I once lived a whole summer season off a whale, and by the time I had finished with it, I was fed up enough."

The Capture of a Whale at Gorleston
(Described by an eye-witness)

The eye-witness was, of course, Arthur. What an exciting event it must have been to see a whale in Yarmouth Harbour. It was 1891 and few people knew anything about whales except that which they had seen in books. The whale was a seven-ton, 30ft. Lesser Rorqual Whale that became bemused by the sandbanks off Yarmouth and found its way into the mouth of the river Yare. The story was described in a pamphlet written by Arthur for the whale's first appearance in London at the Royal Agricultural Hall, Islington, and described as *"a sight once seen, never forgotten."*

On Monday, June the 8th, 1891, I was taking a stroll along the Yarmouth South Denes, towards the Pier, at Gorleston. Coming near this grand old Pier, my attention was arrested by seeing some lifeboatmen hurriedly manning a small boat and making their way in haste out of the river, towards the end of the Pier, which forms the mouth of Yarmouth Harbour. Crowds of people were rushing down to the Pier; to witness a scene such as had never happened here before. Observing this excitement, I said to a young friend of mine, "Harry, what's up, have they some life to save?" "I don't know," said he, "let us run." In great haste we ran to witness, with scores of others, the first known scene of the capture of a Rorqual Whale, in the river Yare, at Gorleston.

As one who has been much interested in the grand and noble work of these brave life-boatmen, I now speak of their courageous spirit, which was manifested in this hazardous calling of capturing so great a sea monster. I saw this huge animal rise upon a great wave, and with tremendous force blowing up water in the air, again diving out of sight and then coming to the surface, with its immensely powerful propeller it smashed its nose by running foul of the Pier head. The crushed nose quickly impregnated the water with blood.

The boatmen, with quick discerning eyes and muscles strong, rowed after it, and approaching the monster with iron creepers and boathooks, made small inflictions, thus driving it up the river.

Again it dashed itself against the quay-head, when these Lifeboatmen, with great dexterity, drove it between the "dolphins" on the South Denes side of the river.

Here they manfully succeeded with ropes, chains and boathooks, in making it fast, the blood as yet freely flowing from its wounds. In about an hour, as the tide went down, it succumbed to the injuries it had received.

At seven o'clock the same evening, several hundreds of the villagers, townsfolk and visitors, crowded the quay near to the Gorleston Volunteer Lifeboat House, expecting to see it raised from the water.

At this juncture, the Lifeboat "Elizabeth Simpson," was launched from its stocks out of the shed of this Volunteer Company (better known as the Ranger Company), to make room for the prize, which they had gained, "The Gorleston Whale."

However, these men, who believe in making the best of everything, did not just then allow the enormous animal to be seen, but as the captors of the whale, they left it below the water and went away.

The crowds returned to their homes greatly disappointed. Shortly afterwards when fewer people were near, they reappeared, and with the use of the powerful Lifeboat windlass, they drew the large Whale of 7 tons into the shed.

Arthur" attending" the Whale in the Gorleston Lifeboat Shed
Courtesy Great Yarmouth Mercury Photographic Archive

A poem was written (author unknown) in celebration of the Gorleston Whale.

The Gorleston Whale

'Twas on the eighth of June, eighteen hundred and ninety one,
The apartment-letting season had scarcely yet begun;
When a monster Rorqual Whale,
Thirty feet from head to tail,
Gave the gallant Gorleston lifeboatmen some work, some gold and fun.

First of all, he tried his strength upon our good old pier,
Which gave unto his poor old nose appearance rather queer;
When the tide was at full flood
And the water tinged with blood,
He plump upon the "dolphins" struck, which then to him were near.

First appear our lifeboatmen, who soon this whale did see,
There's Woods, J. Paston, Whiley, Drane, all men who plough the seas,
Four Flemings and S. Leggett,
And J. Farman, Newson, Rivett,
To kill this wandering monster bold, and chain him to the quay.

Quick the lifeboat is launched out, just as the clock strikes eight,
Many with their little ones that night stayed out quite late;
Job Woods then gave directions,
With many interjections,
J. Paston is appointed to take the money at the gate.

Visitors had now subscribed a handsome little pile,
The faces of the lifeboatmen wore a heavenly smile,
Helped by the men who caught 'im,
The doctors held "post mortem,"
Many came from Norwich city, that's from here full twenty mile.

By use of disinfectants, no smell did one assail,
So fair dames came, and children too, whoever weak and frail;
This fish is worth a visit,
'Tis not much, you won't miss it,
Then you can say, when far away, that you've seen "The Gorleston Whale".

The Rorqual Whale - A Slit Nose

A paragraph appeared in the Yarmouth Mercury on Saturday, June 20th, 1891. The whale, it said, had been the principal theme for conversation during the whole of last, and the early portions of this, week.

On Thursday it was dissected by Mr Shipley, Junior, of Southtown, when Drs. Bately, Blake and Tipple, Messrs. Watts, A Patterson, Southwell, and a number of ladies and gentlemen from Norwich, Lowestoft, Yarmouth and Gorleston were present. The dissection lasted some considerable time, the flesh and entrails being carted away to a boat and sold for dog meat, manure, and so on. The skin was about an inch and a half thick; little fat was to be seen. The operation was a rather difficult one, and the odour of the carcase was anything but pleasant. It proved to be an adult Lesser Rorqual or pike-headed whale, a fine specimen of the *Mysticete* group, known to science as the *Balaenoptera Rostrata*. Its measurements were as follows: - Length, 30 feet; girth, 18 feet; span of tail, 8ft. 2 in.; length of pectoral fins, 4ft. 6 in.; length of jaws, 6ft. 6 in.

Mr Arthur Patterson, in the course of a lecture on the Lesser Rorqual Whale, said that they were of an extraordinary family, warm-blooded, suckle their young, and were air-breathers. Their limbs are modified into fish-like extremities, they live in water, and speedily die when taken from the water, they are animals, mammals in anatomical features and faculties. Whales are of numerous species, they spread all over the globe, and vary in size from six to eighty feet.

The cylindrical form of their captive took off the idea of vastness of its size, and the long and tapering tail aided in this result.

A neck seemed out of the question, the body was smooth and hairless, the under parts smooth and marble-like, corrugated or furrowed, hence its second name of "furrowed" whale. It had a dorsal or back fin; the tail or caudal fin, which was gristly, was horizontally placed, not perpendicular as in a fish. This tail was muscular and solid, immensely powerful, and propelled its owner forward at a high rate.

Quibble as folk do as to whether the egg preceded the hen or vice versa, they could be sure that the naval engineer borrowed an idea or two for his screw propeller from the cetacean. The eye was comparatively small, the ear orifice very diminutive, the fore limbs, termed "flippers", were broadened and flattened, the free part of the hand being coated with a stiff, nail-less membrane. There were no hind limbs, but pelvis bones were found at the setting of the tail. The brain was of considerable size, and greatly convoluted, the heart very large, as were also the lungs. The nostrils opened on the top of the head. Murie, speaking of the breathing and eating process, said: "In front of the larynx of man we all know is an elastic lid, the epiglottis which folds over and protects the air passage as food is swallowed. The side cartilages constitute the walls of the organ of voice, and protect the vocal chords. Now, in the comparatively voiceless whale the cartilages, including the epiglottis, form a long, rigid cylindrical tube, which is thrust up the passage at the back of the palate in continuity of the blowhole. It is there held in place by a muscular ring with the larynx thus retained bolt upright, and the blowhole meanwhile being compressed or closed, the cetacean is enabled to swallow food under water without the latter entering the lungs. Respiration "blowing" or "spouting" takes place at intervals as the animal reaches the surface, and the volume of air thrown up along the surrounding moisture, and condensed vapour in some, rises in a great jet. Whales were of two groups, toothed or *denticete*, and whalebone or *mysticete*. The whale in question was furnished with baleen or whalebone, exceeding a foot in depth in places. In the lower jaw a bog pouch-like fleshy development was capable of containing a large quantity of water and marine animals. The tongue was free. The blubber was not very thick, and the oil from it not of much repute.

The Norwegians have turned their attention to this and the larger relative, the common or greater Rorqual, which is of a maximum length of 70 feet.

These whales feed on *medusae* or jellyfishes, herrings, etc, and even chase salmon. Dogfish are found in the stomach at times. It is a native of the Arctic Seas, American and European coasts, and visits Norway and Iceland. As a visitor to the Norfolk coast it is very rare. In 1829, one is stated to have been cast ashore at Cromer, length 24 feet. In November 1860, an adult whale was stranded on Overstrand Beach, 24 feet long. Its skeleton was presented to the Royal College of Surgeons. The last whale exhibited here measured 45 feet in length, coming ashore at Winterton, January 1857. Visitors were asked to step inside its jaws.

Mr. Thomas Southwell of Norwich gave a supplementary lecture, stating that he had the pleasure of finding out a history attached to the whalebone seat in St. Nicholas' Parish Church, which had been published. The Greenland whale had never visited this Gorleston coast, nor would it, as it did not leave the frozen seas, where its particular food was abundant.

Both lecturers were enthusiastically applauded. During the dissection, Mr. Shipley's knife slipped and cut the cartilage of one of the nostrils of a visitor, who was too close to the whale. Dr. Edwin Tipple and Dr. Blake gave their prompt attention to the injury. The whale has been purchased by Messrs. Joseph J. Cockrell, Woods, and Whiley, who intend having it preserved; this work has been undertaken by W. Lowne, Naturalist, of Fuller's Hill, Great Yarmouth, who will mount it ready for exhibition by Christmas next.

Dr. R. G. Bately held the occasion a fitting one on which to perform a pleasing duty. It will be remembered that we had the pleasure of publishing a heroic act of a man named Adams, who saved a child from a watery grave last year, by diving from the end of the pier. We then intimated that the "pier hero" was deserving of a Royal Humane Society Medal. This the Society concurred with, and he and another man named Spurgeon, as plucky and fearless as the other, both received this award. Both men have saved several lives and deserve the appreciation of the whole parish.

During a spell of unemployment, Arthur travelled with the whale to London, where it was displayed in the Royal Agricultural Hall, Islington. It was returned to Norwich and the lifeboat crew hired Arthur to act as attendant in an empty shop in Norwich market place. Following a successful "stay" the "Wandering Whale" was loaded onto a draycart on June 8th, 1892 to be taken to Lowestoft where it was to be "housed" in a canvas booth in the market place. Arthur described the journey in a letter to the *Eastern Daily Press*. In it, he said:

How the people turned out to see the travelling whale! Sundry were the comments passed upon it. "Twor the biggest thing in the whald!" a "shark," a "summat," or else "twor summat else!" The urchins trotted by us, and one youngster in particular, with a tom-tit nest in his hand – a naturalist, I'll warrant, in embryo – plied us with questions, and amused us with answers to our own.

And thus we trudged along, using our eyes to the best advantage until we reached Lowestoft, which we entered scarcely able to see at all, for we were smothered with dust from head to foot, and not a little of it had found its way into our optics, for the roads were dusty, and the horses with their great hoofs churned it up in little clouds! The journey took twelve hours.

After a spell in Lowestoft, the Whale went on its final journey to Yarmouth to be exhibited on the seafront for the summer season, hence Arthur completing a year of living off a whale!

Chapter 12
THE CAISTER LIFEBOAT DISASTER

A Supplement to the *"Yarmouth Mercury"* was issued on Saturday, November 23rd, 1901. Priced at 1d. it was published by the Great Yarmouth Printing Company Ltd., Theatre Plain. The front cover was designed by Arthur Patterson, and inside were pictures of the wreck of the *"Beauchamp"* and subsequent funeral of the men who died. Although not written by Arthur Patterson, the sad story, told in a poem by W. A. Osborne, deserves a place here.

Front Cover of Yarmouth Mercury supplement, November 23rd, 1901

Wreck of the Caister Lifeboat, Thursday, November 14th, 1901

> *Hark, through the howling tempest,*
> *Comes the sound of a warning bell,*
> *That terrible summons to duty,*
> *Which mothers and wives know well;*
> *Somewhere a ship is in danger,*
> *Out on the treacherous sands,*

'Tis a call for "The Lifeboat", listen !
The coxswain wants all hands.

In spite of the heavy breakers,
In spite of the warning gale,
These brave men launched the "Beauchamp",
While the women grew faint and pale;
Ploughing their way by inches,
They reached where the vessel lay,
But their task in the end was fruitless,
They could give no help that day.

Battered and disappointed,
Those who had perilled their lives,
Steered through the gloomy darkness,
Back to their homes and wives;
Just on the shore had they grounded,
When a huge wave bearing down.,
Dashed in its fury upon them,
Tossing them high on its crown.

Swiftly the boat keeled over,
Well might men set their teeth,
Those who so lately had manned her,
In a second lay caged beneath.
Closed as it were a coffin,
Bruised by the water's might,
Only to "three" was it granted,
To live through that ghastly night.

"Nine" in discharge of their duty,
Died, and are gone to their rest.
Still, ye bereaved ones who sorrow,
Remember the Lord knows best.
He hath looked down on their toiling,
Mid the elements' storm and strife,
And death through His infinite mercy,
May prove but the gate of Life.

Chapter 13
CHARLES HARMONY HARRISON

"Our efforts were rewarded in time to push back the shadows that were beclouding the last days of poor Charles' life and let in a bit of sunshine."

Arthur Smith, a fellow naturalist friend, teamed up with Arthur to write a memoir of their friend, Charles Harrison, *C. H. Harrison, Broadland Artist*. It was published in 1903, limited to 175 copies, and profits from the sale of the book were added to the fund to provide for his widow and children. Like Arthur, Harrison was a boy from the Rows at Yarmouth.

Dawn

Charles was born in a dingy house in Row 33 in January 1842. Fortunately, his parents later moved to a cottage on St. Nicholas' Road, with a brighter outlook, and there the boy developed his love of the beautiful and soon gave promise of unusual artistic powers. He attended the Congregational Day School in Middlegate Street, where he worked hard but was not favoured by his schoolmaster.

A kindred spirit was discovered in Samuel W. Bond, and together the school friends passed their leisure hours in the study of Botany and Natural History. His nature notes were occasionally illustrated from life, and the few early drawings by him showed how keenly he observed even the humble offerings of nature.

He left school early and went to work for Thomas Olley for a while, then was awarded an apprenticeship with Mr. Platt, a sign-writer and decorator, in Row 45. It was not long before he was recognised as an accomplished writer and decorator. There he acquired confidence in the use of colours. In all his work as a decorator his love of detail was noticeable, although he was a very rapid worker. He painted portraits, animals, and sea-scapes, but was highly critical of himself and destroyed his work when he discovered faults in it. Mr. G. Calver, F.R.A.S., another Yarmouth artist, encouraged him to persevere. Harrison was fond of drawing ideal landscapes for his friends' amusement, and although the drawings were crude and somewhat faulty in colour, the conceptions were bold and distinguished by the features characteristic of the accomplished artist. Still water, lilies, and reflections were always conspicuous, while his trees, even then, were exceptionally faithful.

Charles Harmony Harrison

Early Struggles

Harrison was a companionable young man, brimming with energy and patriotism; he joined the Yarmouth Artillery Volunteers in May 1859. His master, however, objected to military associations, so Harrison resigned his apprenticeship. Discontented, he soon afterwards joined the Rifle Volunteers, and continued for many years as a member, eventually becoming a sergeant. His interest in military matters was keen, and he won the notice and friendship of comrades and superiors. He married in 1866 Miss Edith Porter, and to supplement his earnings from his paintings, he worked as a grainer and sign-writer. In 1872 he received his first commission, and the result was a drawing of Old Ramp Row. It produced seven shillings and sixpence. Encouraged at receiving further commissions he decided, for better or for worse, he would be an artist: to paint the scenes around him, and win a name with drawings of a district then comparatively unknown. His own style was soon formed. In 1876-7 Lady Crossley of Somerleyton, purchased several fine drawings by Harrison. Charmed with their beauty, she invited many of her friends to examine them. One of them, Walter Goodhall, the art dealer, was keen to know more about the rising Yarmouth artist.   Harrison was invited to visit Somerleyton, taking with him some of his pictures and to meet Mr. Goodhall. A visit followed, and many delightful days were spent at Somerleyton Hall, where Harrison was a welcome guest of Lady Crossley.

With pencil and sketch-book

A little while passed, and Harrison knew his first great sorrow. His young wife died after a long illness, leaving two children to remind him of a loss too great for words or tears.   He sought consolation in work, and found it. Many beautiful sketches of scenes by the wayside showed how patiently he sought for neglected corners worthy of his pencil and brush; but the sunshine and the glow which entered into so much of his later work failed at this period to inspire him; all the charm was there, but the tone was occasionally depressing and suggestive of a man whose buoyancy had departed.

As time went on he extended his journeys, and the charms of the Waveney attracted him. The quaint old world appearance of Beccles from the river was reproduced with many effects, and several studio drawings of the bridge and the neighbouring scenery were sold to well-known art patrons. Excursions to Beccles in time became yet more pleasurable with the advent of a new attraction. Harrison, grown tired of a companionless life, followed Cupid again, and found favour with a lady who frequently visited a sister then residing in the town. A few miles of country were not allowed to interfere with the course of true love, and his ardent wooing soon won a response, which invited him to look once more on the brighter side of life. He married on the February 11th, 1878, Miss Emma Read, the daughter of a well-known Yarmouth tradesman, and departed at once for London.

Previous to this, Harrison had formed the acquaintance of Stephen Batchelder, a brother artist, who painted delightful pictures of Broadland and East Coast scenery. A chance meeting at Corton, where Batchelder was sketching a wreck, was followed by many journeys together, and a kindred feeling being fostered by joint service in the Rifle Volunteers, and mutual esteem, ripened into friendship, which continued almost unbroken to the end. Harrison was unable to settle in London, and deplored living in "the muddy hole" he described his house as, at 3, Percy Terrace, Acacia Road, Wood Green. Unceasing work produced sufficient for comfort, but with the coming of summer he longed for a sketching tour with his friend Batchelder or Calver, but the needs of his home left him without the necessary means. Mrs. Harrison endeavoured to supply his need of a critic, but with the best will in the world to be impartial, she rarely succeeded.

Broadland

In March 1879, Harrison prepared to return to Yarmouth. He had learned much during his exile, and frequent meetings with famous artists in London increased his desire to apply his knowledge. In the summer of 1880, Harrison and Batchelder spent a sketching tour on the River Bure and its tributaries, by rowing boat and picturesque "Noah's Ark" houseboat. Two years later he secured his well-known boat *"Psyche"*, and in this he proceeded to discover yet more nooks and corners of his beloved Broads. These were Harrison's halcyon days, but the rewards, apparently great, little more than sufficed for his needs. There was no hope of ultimate fortune or comparative ease, yet Harrison did not lose heart. His contributions to East Anglian Exhibitions, and the Exhibitions of the Royal Institute of Water-Colour Painters, were usually purchased before the opening days, and at Ipswich, Norwich and London, and other places, critics whose reputations were national generously praised his work. Harrison would not exhibit work that did not satisfy him, and even the repeated assurances of the managers of important Art Exhibitions that his contributions would be hung on the line, were insufficient to overcome his scruples. The work of the period 1880 to 1900 was regarded as his best; his strongest and most sympathetic work certainly appears in drawings done during the eighties.

Lengthening Shadows

Long after increasing deafness had begun to make him more and more reclusive in his habits, his eye and hand had not as yet flagged in their grasp and delineation of Broadland scenery, but the feeling of isolation and lonesomeness grew upon him apace, and he felt keenly the disadvantages it placed him under. He mixed less and less with his old associates, and remained longer in his studio. Necessity kept him busily employed with the brush - there were yet several little ones whose upbringing taxed his resources to the utmost; and at a period when most men look to have their families in a fair way for self-support there were still toddlers around the hearth.

There were weeks and months of intermittent ill-health, when only a little good work was done. When Harrison began to realise that the vigour of his early and magnificent manhood was on the wane, he began to lose heart, and originality, and forcefulness. Commissions still came in for good work, but he did not feel himself equal to it, and gradually disappointment made his patrons fall off one by one. A few months before the end Harrison's powers and abilities began rapidly to flag, and fits of depression and "nerves" would come over him, and he would sit for hours reading and ruminating. His energies diminished and he would make fitful efforts at picture making when the household needs made more than passing demand for supplies. Sketches were begun and thrown aside; the inspiration died away before its dream was realised. His right hand began to lose freedom of movement and he would remark with sorrow: *"I'm past it now!"* and taking off his glasses to brush away a tear, acknowledge his work had about come to an end. Rheumatism and loss of nerve-power grew upon him quickly, and the strong mind lost its vigour.

After the "stroke", Harrison for a while rallied, but had laid aside brush and paint-box for good and all. As the dust gathered upon his tools he fretted himself. It was pitiful to see the great man led about his room by his patient wife's aid, and he soon became so helpless that she had to assist him even to light his pipe.

On their removal to Churchill Road, Yarmouth, still more sketches had to go; indeed his portfolios now had regularly to keep things going. It was at this time that he became reminiscent, and bit by bit told many of the incidents that marred or brightened his career. As his weakness increased he became more cheery; he even went so far as to have his fishing-rods done up and placed in a corner of his room *"ready for next season"*, and would talk of what he hoped to do again on the Broads when health and spring returned.

In the late autumn, just before the leaves had commenced to fall, and while the country lanes were yet beautiful, a great longing came over Harrison to see his beloved Broads again. He was a prisoner upstairs, and could only slouch from chair to chair with help; he could not stand alone. It would be no small task to get such a big-framed ailing man like him downstairs, even without the additional excitement and risk of a country drive. But it came about. Unexpectedly one afternoon, a vehicle drove up to the door and two of his friends (myself and Arthur Smith) called in to take him. He was asleep, and dishevelled. He hesitated, stair by stair, step by step, an inch or two at a time - got into the trap.

Poor fellow! How he brightened up as the wheels scrunched along the roadway and presently reached the main road, and how eagerly did the great lustrous eyes take in old familiar scenes as they rumbled along - the big brown wherry-sail marked out the course of the river Bure, the hawthorns and firs held out their cones and berries as if to welcome him again, and the rooks wheeling overhead were not the first by many hundreds that had caught his eye as he sketched the lowlands in the old days. Everything that he looked on reminded him of the balmier days of his rambling, and he tried hard to obliterate the starting tear with a grateful smile as it stole between his vision and the vista before him, and would blur the landscape. Here and there, as Caister, Ormesby, and other villages were passed, spots made historic by the creations of his brush were pointed out, and incident and anecdote relating to that work were narrated. He was depressed only when turning his eye across the rippling Broads that so many times had borne him on their bosom.   Did he not realise, poor fellow! that this surely must be - as it was - his last time of drinking in their beauties? The last occasion of his ever being near them.

For a month or two after that he was cheery and gossipful; the visits went on for a while longer, and that pathetic excursion was always touched upon. But the shadows crept on; the sun was dipping below the horizon.

Night

On October 4th, 1902, a letter appeared in the local papers calling attention in a roundabout way to Harrison's gloomy circumstances, and suggested that an exhibition of his pictures would not only be a fitting compliment to his genius, but probably lead to more tangible marks of esteem and appreciation, as well as become a source of great pleasure to many of his fellow-townsmen.

The letter, written by Arthur Patterson, deplored the fact that the Tolhouse Museum and Art Gallery did not possess a single drawing of Harrison's.

This letter was promptly followed by another, which strongly backed up the suggestion to secure drawings by the Museum Committee; and urged the organisation of a Loan Exhibition of Pictures. Within a month an exhibition was opened to the public but whilst efforts were being made to promote it, on November 13th, 1902, Harrison died. He was sixty. The exhibition, however, raised sufficient funds to provide Harrison's widow with a small weekly allowance for several years.

On November 19th, 1902 on a bright, clear, crisp morning, while the surf on the seashore thundered a not unfitting requiem to one whose soul had loved the rippling Broadland waters, Charles Harrison was laid to rest in the Yarmouth Cemetery, amid many manifestations of regard and numerous tributes of public sympathy and respect... The six coffin bearers were all colour-sergeants of the 2nd V.B.N.R., comrades of the deceased artist, and their scarlet coats suffused the last pathetic scenes with a welcome ray of colour. This guard of honour, as it might almost be termed, comprised Colour-Sergeants Emerson, Beckett, Lamb, Batchelder (retired), Buddery (retired), and Maystone (retired). The artists of Yarmouth, the anglers, and members of the local authorities, were all present to do homage to the genius of his brush, that has given us so many lovely scenes and bestowed fame on our delightful Broadland!

On the following day another appreciation appeared in the *Eastern Daily Press;* it was Arthur's tribute to his old friend.

A Last Tribute

Yesterday, under a cold, clear, sunlit sky, without the suggestion of a cloud above-head, and in the presence of a goodly gathering of old admirers and acquaintances, was laid to rest all that was mortal of Charles Harmony Harrison, the painter lad who had once placed as honest sweeps of colouring upon door and palisade as did the man grown put faithful delineations from nature on board and canvas, and whose pencil scorned to tell an unspoken lie. It was fitting that those who had been taught to love more and more the beauty around them should drop a tear into the clean yellow sand-hummocks that margined the grave wherein they placed their respected dead; and right genuine were the whispered eulogies that passed from friend to friend as they turned for the last time to mark the spot where the genius of the Broadlands sleeps. And as sincere, we hope, will be their resolve to do justice to the merits of the departed artist.

There was one little incident that seemed appropriate - the placing of a bunch of fresh-gathered rushes and reed-tufts, and faded reed mace, sometimes called the bulrush, on the coffin lid of the dead. It seemed fitting that at least the characteristic flora of the Broads, whose beauties have been so faithfully and so often illustrated in the creations of his pencil, should be represented amid the tenderer floral tributes that hid, here and there, the graining of the casket. It was seemly, too, that they were tied together by one whom, perhaps, in other ways, loves the Broadlands almost as well as he did. Could the rustle of the sere and curling leaves have but penetrated to the deaf ears beneath, Harrison could not have desired a more comely token, or more appropriate offering, simple as it might be. His favourite lilies were not there, for are not last summer's flower gems faded, and dropped into the bosom of the Broads that bore them?

It was mine to visit the dead genius as he lay, as if in sleep, in the chamber of his departure. It had been mine, rarely, to smooth out the rumple in the uneasy pillow of a fading little one; but it is a rarer sorrow and privilege to look upon the face of a departed genius. There were two of us who looked on him - two fellows as antithetic as you could well find in Yarmouth for companionship (that is, Arthur, himself, and Arthur Smith). There, under the softening flicker of the lamp held in the trembling hand of a faithful wife - the widow, the noble, marble-white face of poor Harrison bore a look of silent, contented triumph. We sent poor Charles out of the world happy!

The lines, and wrinkles, and creases of care, and anxiety and pain - borne uncomplainingly - had all gone, and in their stead had come back the old complacent smile, such as had crept over these features in life when a drawing, scarcely dry, of some beloved spot had received the last few touches that fixed, once for all, the glory of his completed canvas. Harrison fell on sleep happily and contented, for he knew in time, that a number of his old-time admirers had rallied round him in his hour of need; and among these those who had, to a certain extent, tried meanwhile to lighten his sorrow and to push back the gathering gloom which fortunately had passed away, like a storm-cloud he sometimes threw into a Broadland landscape. The squall went by in time, and Charles, who had dreaded to die poor, just saw the sun shining over the edging, as you know it oft-times does; and you have seen the sunlight sweeping along over the rain-sparkled herbage,

"Chasing far the gloom and terror,
Brightening all the path we tread,"

until there had been only sufficient greyness above the horizon remaining as a fitting background to throw up the nearer objects into happy relief. So Harrison just lived to see the rift in the cloudland; he drank in the cheery rays that broke through - and died. His work was finished, his fears had been banished, and he passed quietly away to his rest.

There have been people who have lived a long life, and died old, having accomplished - nothing. Others crowd into a space far less than the allotted three score years and ten a busy full life's work. Just so, Harrison left the world better than he found it, and many a home is the brighter for his loving labours. Show me the man who spends himself for others, and who, dying young, peradventure, has completed life's work well. Such would I myself be rather. It must be pleasant to feel one lives to make this old world the richer for our living. Harrison left something behind him; his many pictures will live on and increase in value as his work becomes more deservedly appreciated. Harrison also left some little ones behind him; let us not forget them for his sake.

One other word: Harrison loved nature with all the instincts and ardour of a born naturalist. In earlier life he rambled with a most capable botanist. As his days grew shorter and his feebleness increased, it was his delight to tell many a reminiscent fact about the living creatures which shared the solitudes of Broadland with him; of the birds that unexpectedly fluttered into his kindly presence; of the fish that darted away at his shadow and hid in their reed-shaded hollows; of the bright-winged insects that danced around him as he painted, hesitant, mayhap, whether they had not a right to alight upon a yet wet spray of purple loosestrife or pink willow-herb, or a reed-mace standing out in bold relief in the foreground of a sketch upon his easel. He would talk of these until one felt that a naturalist might sometimes be an artist, and that an artist must necessarily be a naturalist. But the artist, like his fellows, must die, and what fitter good-bye offering could be than that bunch of Broadland weeds, gathered at Filby, to which was attached an equally befitting epigram:

"From one of his well-beloved Broads - to be buried with him."

"Autumn Glory". A painting by Charles Harrison

Chapter 14
AN AMATEUR ARTIST AMONG THE BIRDS

"Wallis took us for walks in the country on Friday afternoons in summer, and when it was wet, or in winter, he used to stand me on a stool to draw sketches for the other kiddies' amusement."

When I was a small kiddie trotting about with loaves of bread, potatoes, and trifles of that sort - I dawdled a great deal, through peering into picture-frame shops, and into windows where old water- and oil-colours were exposed to view - revelling in land and water, hungrily wishing that such beautiful things could come into my own little world and life. My first penny-box of rubbishy paints - made I presume of blueing bag stuff and brick dust, *"Made in Germany",* of course, rather set the old folks against what I thought would improve the woodcuts in the household books. What mischief I might have done had I obtained Rowney's or Reeve's tubes of colour, I almost dread now to think of.

I might have been 9 years old, when I, one day, trotted behind my Dad into the old churchyard, where his lost treasures lay buried. The beauty of some little trees bewitched me; and I told him that some day I wanted to be an artist, and paint them. "Goodness, boy! Nothing of the kind," said he, "that's only a lazy man's hobby. Work - boy - work!"

So I got few paints and brushes; and not then having read of Sir Benjamin West's cutting sable-hair off his cat's tail, I was stowed up a corner; besides if I had done so, my stepmother's wrath at my so mutilating her cat, would have put such nonsense out of my head on the instant.

Perhaps father was right in squashing me, for a boy of nine, although he may possess certain instincts, is usually changeable as a weathercock. I am afraid I was, for when the next menagerie came to town I wanted to start one. And then I had the naturalist's craze for sticklebacks and snakes - I got it like the measles - badly. For all these impulses Father had one remedy - work, for what did the Bible say - wasn't man to earn his bread by the sweat of his brow? I did sweat - for years, for a bare existence. My thick hands show it to this day.

Now, the oddest thing of all was this - that I have had all my wishes fulfilled, to an extent, since I was getting my living among monkeys and lions - a poor living too, I admit: as a field naturalist all my life, have I been; and as for being an artist, I have been an amateur artist.

Perhaps Father made three mistakes in his life: first he let me visit the menagerie without protest, as my poor brother William was a friend of Macomo's, the beast tamer in Mander's Menagerie; secondly, he (my Dad) used to drive me in state on top of the manure barrow to the allotment garden, where a dead rat set the ball rolling for my nature-work, and thirdly - Father having once seen me carve a man's face out of a block of stone - the sort he used to saw up for step cleaning - praised my work, the only time that I can recall when he ever did such a thing. The Black Macamo, the rat, the stone face, I can see today as plainly as I saw them then.

As a kiddie of nine, my old schoolmaster William Wallis early discovered in me the bents of my mind, and fostered my propensities. It was a poor school, but an excellent master - and what little education I possess I greatly owe to him. Well, he took us walks into the country on Friday afternoons in summer, and when it was wet, or in winter, he used to stand me on a stool to draw sketches for the other kiddies' amusement.

We were taught freehand drawing twice weekly. Copies were chalked, or pinned on the board; and we did our work on those abominable slates of the 1860's. We boys sat six on a form, to reproduce some grotesque thing. We had so many marks, to pile up against the quarterly small reward. Having no pupil teachers, our poor old mentor would take advantage of the drawing lesson, to attend to some other class. Consequently, when left alone, we had a high old time: two lads in my class owned fathers who were herring curers; so they would fill their pockets with red herrings, and when at drawing lesson would cut them into sections and hand round, creating an odour that had "an ancient and fish-like smell" of the Dickenses' variety. Naturally these refreshments greased our fingers and also the slates, which became so oily, as well as did the pencils, that inscriptions on the slates became as drawn in a fog-bank; and moreover, when the boys breathed upon the slates, it was like a Scotch mist. We held up slates when ordered, with bated breath. Without being a freak in any way, my slate was usually the most legible, and was probably the most worthy of commendation. But the boys never resented this when no punishment ensued, and I would keep them cheery by making comical sketches of the master and the class. Later on we rose to paper, pencil and India rubber.

In 1878, I started to add authorship to my love of nature, and in time discovered that an ability to make a rough sketch added interest not only to my own notebooks, but also to my readers. I happily thought of a process of colouring my sketches; first I very roughly pencilled an idea, then I used a saucer with a spoonful of water, in which I dropped a little Indian ink. With a fine brush I outlined and shaded my figures. This dried almost instantly; if it did not, it mattered little. Then I put a dinner-spoonful of turpentine into another saucer, and squeezed out four or five oil colours, chiefly red, blue, green, yellow and brown, upon the palate or upon the top edge of the saucer. Then I dipped a medium sable into the turps, took up a little colour, and rapidly spread the colour on, and over the inked lines. The picture becomes dry the moment you have finished it - and the turps that spreads a little quickly dries out. These drawings, thus made show well by gaslight; and are very convenient for illustrating a lecture. Besides, a sketch does not cost more than the fraction of a farthing! And moreover, they are transparent and with a light behind can be seen as easily as by daylight.

These rough cartoons took but a few minutes each to do, but on good paper, with a little care, a turpentine drawing looks quite as well as a watercolour.

When as a youth, I offered an article to the late Mr. Spellings, he held up his index finger and remarked; *"Look here, Patterson, when you write for the Press tell the folks what they already know, they'll like it all the better!"* I thought this out, and found he was right; why, look how even lady artists rush for the paper to read all about yesterday's wedding - how the bride looked, and wept, how the bridegroom smiled, and blushed, and how they were dressed - and they'd seen all of it themselves!

The same argument applied I think to pictures - how Norfolk picture lovers will have Broadland scenes upon their walls; how rarely do you see moorland hills, and rocky glens on Norfolk walls. You cherish their reflexes because you know them. And how few indulge in impressionist work - preferring truthfulness to overheated impressions that land you into artistic fog and obscure situations

Personally, I love Art and I love Nature; they are twin sisters - they love and help each other. They do not quarrel, although Art, who was the second born, occasionally fails to show all her sister's most beautiful emotions; indeed, Nature bears with her sister's little failings; and is always eager that she should try again.   For one thing I am sorry. How few artists - amateur and professional - does one see about our street corners today. It may be that the rage for cleansing our old towns, and knocking out all the quaintness, the colour, and the romance of the old days, to make so-called improvements has something to do with this.

I know, as a kiddie, I used to shyly edge up to folks who sat on little campstools, and sucked brushes, and make all sorts of queer mystic signs in the air, with thumb and pencil, and stand spellbound as the colours conjured up from old buildings in which I had, probably, never before, seen any beauty at all.

Once a handsome, elderly man sat in front of the North West Tower near the Yacht Station; he was transferring it in miniature to his easel, stone by stone, brick by brick; when suddenly to my surprise, he popped in a sickly, green tree, where there was none.

"Sir," I said, rather impulsively, *"but there ain't a tree!"*

He looked up at me, and was at once sympathetic, *"Of course there isn't,"* said he, *"but, my boy, that's put in by an artist's licence!"* I remember puzzling over the remark; I knew what a pedlar's certificate, or hawker's licence was, but a picture-licence seemed a queer qualification.

I am not the only one who has misconstrued ethical matters. Wrote a Yarmouth musician teacher to a rich tradesman who could scarcely sign his own name*: "Dear Sir, you are wasting time and money over your daughter's music lessons. She will never succeed; she has no talent for it."*

The Dad was surprised and ordered his clerk to reply. *"Madam, if she has no talent, she must have some; get it for her, no matter the cost of it…"*

There seems to me today to be a slump in art; people who should encourage the artist freely spend their money on that which is not art, and fail to appreciate those who try to make life and home beautiful by transferring the beauties of the landscape into their homes. Perhaps we may have a revival some day. If you went among the homes of the poor, as I do, you would be appalled by the want of beauty apparent. A table up one side of a room, with a few pieces of common glass, ugly ornaments, and few dusty books; on the walls, perhaps, one or two dilapidated oleographs, and faded photographs. In some not even these, but the wallpaper hanging in strips. The only hope I have for raising the ideals of another generation is in the schools, which might, and must be, made brighter by things that are beautiful; and the children of the poor should be taken to picture galleries, as some, better off, are taken to museums. I have tried to get poor folk to grow nasturtiums, and cheap flowers on their windowsills to give a bit of brightness, but it is a dragging effort - as yet as ever, the poor do not appreciate things artistic.

The late Charles Harrison was painting in the open. Said a fellow, who sidled up to him:

"Dear me! Just fancy a grate hulkin' fellow like you, wastin' yer time over doin' rubbish like that ere!" Fortunately, for him he had seen enough and walked on. Another one came to him and said a similar thing, with slightly more emphasis - when up jumped Charles, and landed him a big fist between the eyes, and told him to go to a place that is rarely spoken of nowadays outside of a Salvation Army meeting.

Said Mr. Porkum, the sausage-maker, to an artist friend, who was showing him his masterpiece: *"So ye did that, did yer?"*

"Yes," replied the artist, *"and I have received £1,000 for it."*

"Great Scott," said Mr. Porkum. *"Now you'll be able to quit paintin' and go into sum kind o' business, won't yer?"*

Amateur criticism is not always flattering, as no doubt some of you have experienced.

"I've seen a good many people painters about here," said a boy who was looking over the shoulder of an artist.

"Then you must be quite a critic, I suppose," said the artist.

"Oh no, I ain't ser," answered the boy, *"I keep my opinions to meself!"*

I never had any lessons in drawing, but two very short ones, since I finished with the old slates at day school. Once Mr. Frank Southgate wrote me a five-page letter on perspective; and the other was a suggestion from Mr. Stephen Batchelder as to drawing a boat.

I would say that my frequent chalking on the blackboard in schools, which I visit, has been a little help towards improvement; and a readiness on my part to hear gratuitous grumblings proffered me by those who are my betters, has not been wasted.

Stephen Batchelder, Broadland artist

A year or so ago, a well known Midland naturalist, who recently advocated a memorial window to Gilbert White, in Selborne church, Hampshire, wrote a small book on duck decoys. He came to see me and asked me if I would do him half-a-dozen sketches of ducks and decoys as illustration.

Said he: *"I wrote to --- (our greatest bird painter) asking him if he would paint me a frontispiece to the Duck Decoy Book, telling him that the proceeds were to help towards a memorial to Gilbert White, and thinking he would be only too pleased to do so. But he said he could not do it under £50. Then I asked --- (another world-known bird painter) but he wrote to say he couldn't undertake it under £25. I have to get my living by painting! Then I applied to you, a working man, and you have done six for nothing."*

"More fool you," someone may say; and that amateurs like you spoil better men, but is there not such a thing as doing a thing for love of it!

I didn't even get a presentation copy from the publisher (although it had been agreed upon) until I had had a fortnight's correspondence with him. If I were paid for all I do, I should be pretty well-to-do, for the kiddies in the streets even follow me up with bits of well-thumbed paper, saying: *"Do me a sketch, Mr. Patterson."* And how can one refuse a little kiddie?

A word or two about Yarmouth artists may not be out of place. Of Charles Harrison and Stephen Batchelder I need say little; the first was a genius, but did not pass through the schools. He may have been occasionally a little bit faulty in perspective, but some of his colouring has rarely been excelled. His wherries, yachts, waterlilies, reeds, the very water, they were reflected in was exquisite.

My old friend Batchelder's work Norwich knows well; and in his older years still paints, for I have been with him on a boat sketching trip. At Salhouse I happened to interrupt him when he was engrossed in an inspiration: in an instant he came down to earth and spoke words to me. And were not in Holy Writ. I was in the wrong, I admitted - it was merely a remark I made upon a certain colour aspect - it might have been trivial. He roughly apologised afterwards, but I assured him I was delighted at his pyrotechnic display, as it was bliss to me to see more than one side of a man! For forty-odd years we have been the best of friends. I wish he was not so - always - mathematically correct, and truthful in his painting; his perspective is good, and his representations of Broadland are always sunny.

As a boy I used to delight in W.H. Hart's broad-washes of drawings of Yarmouth Beach and shipping: some of his figure drawing left a little to be desired, but his seascapes were nice. His work fetches little today.

We had some breezy work in watercolour by a man named Neave, if he readily did them, but I have a shrewd suspicion that he only put his name to drawings done by a lunatic in the Royal Naval Asylum (St. Nicholas Hospital) where he - Neave - was a keeper.

Then we had a young man who was an assistant in a draper's shop, where I was a warehouse porter (Palmers Limited, Market Place, Great Yarmouth). We often talked pictures. He could turn wherries, old piles, quaysides into very pretty and effective pictures, and for a time sold fairly well out of Yarmouth. Then his mind must have gone a trifle for he took up impressionist work. I could often see nothing in them and even when he acrobatted backwards and forwards getting certain lights, I still had to be told what they represented. Finally he took up ticket-counting, and, I believe, died, poor chap, with a broken heart and a *bursted* purse. His name was Chamberlain.

Then there appeared in the artistic firmament a new star. I won't mention his name. He painted anything - I sometimes think - anyhow. Trees were proportionately usually three times the proper height. Would I let him paint me and my houseboat? I did, unfortunately. But the owner - myself - came out (proportionately) at 10 feet; the cabin four feet; the mill behind 150 ft. and the grasses were thick enough for faggots.

As a penciller he was excellent. *"For goodness sake,"* I once told him, being a bit critical, I admit, *"don't put a touch of paint on it, or you'll spoil it!"*

Once he opened a barber's shop, making one half of it into a studio. He cut hair almost as well as he painted. One day a half-finished picture stood on his easel. A dove flew on top of it whilst I was looking to see what the picture was.

"Put that thing off!" said I, *"he looks up to some mischief."*

"He's all right," said the artist, *"he often does that!"*

"But he'll make a mess of it!" I insisted and the bird certainly did.

"Don't worry, old boy," insisted the artist, *"that'll all work into the sky!"* and suited his action to his prophesy. Indeed I think it rather improved his sky, which was usually as if done with a whitewash brush. *"And,"* he added, *"if an artist works in a few flies, a picture sells better."*

"Indeed," I said.

"Yes," he went on, *"they naturally think it was done in the open air!"*

Of poor Tobias Lewis, a young Jew friend of mine, who fell in Palestine, I can say but little. His work showed genius and a vast strength and rugged beauty; his *Entry of Smacks into Yarmouth Harbour* in a gale in our Tolhouse is worth looking at; and his *Shepherd and Dog* was a fine picture. He was a charming fellow and I liked him almost as a son.

I should like to tell you of a self-constituted artist in Yarmouth who has lately taken-up oils, but when I assure you that he always seems to see Broadland with cloudless skies; and I once pointed out to him a mill with the shady part painted on what should have been the sunny one, I need say no more.

Let me say how vexing it is to me that so many artists who are good at landscapes are failures at animals and birds: and a land- or waterscape might be occasionally improved by the introduction of a cow, or a seagull, a coot or a heron. One artist introduced bullocks that no sane butcher would have slaughtered without a careful examination of their anatomy!

And unfortunately, some folks who would paint birds do not look at them with a naturalist's eye. Nothing can be more symmetrical and delightfully smooth as velvet and each feather in its place as correctly as squares on a chessboard. I note faults very often in books, especially old books, where the artist was only too true in his copying, possibly from birds badly and inartistically stuffed. Often feathers are puffed out in pictures to create an effect; a mistake often seen in studies in artists' windows. Legs are distorted, or misplaced, wings do not fit, and poses are, to say the least, wretched.

A bird in its growth, takes pattern from the egg it sprang from: and few things in creation are more symmetrically formed than an egg.

How to draw a bird from an egg...

Even a bird stuffer today will make the low body of a bird as nearly a perfect oval as possible. The legs of a bird must always be out in the centre of gravity, or in a picture it looks unsightly; in a stuffed bird it will collapse and fall on his bill, or try to stand on its tail.

Chapter 15
GERALD

I travelled to The Somme, in northern France, in May 2000, to visit the grave of Arthur's youngest son, Gerald Phillips Patterson.

Born in 1897, my great-uncle, Gerald, was the last child of Arthur and Alice, and seemingly their favourite. As a child, Gerald accompanied his father on rambles into the world of nature, loving birds, flowers, fishes and insects. Gerald was intent on following in his father's footsteps and became a keeper in the Insect House at Regent's Park Zoological Gardens in London.

Gerald, Arthur's youngest son, taken in 1897

He met a young London girl called Martha Florence and they became engaged. When war was declared and Gerald joined the army, Florence moved to Great Yarmouth to live with her future mother- and father-in-law. Her health had not been good in London, and her doctor had predicted that moving to the north-sea coast would "kill or cure". Indeed, her health improved.

*Private 43689, Gerald Phillips Patterson, 8th Battalion, Norfolk Regiment,
photographed with his father prior to his posting to France*

Gerald joined the Norfolk Regiment, and on leaving for the Battlefields of France, he told Florence that he did not believe in soldiers marrying before they left for active service. However, something changed, and from the battlefield on the Somme Florence received a letter in which he said he wished they *had* married.

Tragically, on Thursday, October 5th,1916, Gerald was killed in battle at Thiepval, a village about 8 kilometres north-east of Albert.   He is buried in Connaught Cemetery, together with two others from his battalion, Privates 13462 B. Conyers and 22361 F. G. Hanner, who died the same day.

It was not until early in 1917 that Great-Grandfather was informed that Gerald, his naturalist boy, who had been missing since October the previous year, had been killed on The Somme. To keep his mind off his grief, he scribbled *"The Snipe-shooters Club"*. His other four sons all served in khaki, and survived the War: Jack, Gilbert, Arthur and William. His old friend, the bird artist, Frank Southgate, whose paintings illustrate some of his books, also died "hearty and reckless" in France.

Later, after the war, Florence fell in love with and married Gerald's elder brother, John (Jack Patterson).

The Patterson Family. Gerald is seated between his parents.
My grandmother, Helen, is standing behind him.

Gerald's grave in the Connaught Cemetery, Thiepval, France

Chapter 16
CHATS ABOUT THE BIRDIES

"Books are a tremendous help but the true naturalist learns by observation."

This chapter has been chosen from a series written for young naturalists in *"Springtime",* a monthly magazine published by the *Primitive Methodist Publication Company*, 1910 -14.

A talk about beaks

Everything which goes into birds' cupboards - their crops, of course - must go between those curious hard, horny mandibles, which people term the beak. To be correct, a bird has an upper mandible and a lower mandible. You will find in most instances the upper one is the larger and more imposing, the under closing up to it, and apparently, in many cases shutting it. Look at the Parrot's greater curved upper mandible; note the Duck's small flat under one. If you look closely at a bird's bill, or beak, you will find it serves many purposes. The Hawk uses it for a sort of knife and scissors. The Woodpecker uses his as a pair of cutting-pliers with which he chips away the decaying bark of trees in order to find the creatures hidden behind. The Parrot uses his as nutcrackers, and the Duck as a spoon and skimmer. The Curlew's beak might serve for a borer. Look at your hen's beak or bill; does it not serve for hands, mouth, teeth, and even nose? For do you not see the nostrils bored on top? Why, she even uses it as a comb and brush to put her feathers right: and if you put your fingers through the wires she will most likely use it as a fist, and strike at you!

If you ever have a poor dead bird in your hands you will note that these mandibles are moveable, the under one in particular - indeed, in most cases, the upper is fixed. But a Parrot moves both. The muscles are strong which control the lower mandible, and this is so nicely jointed that its movements are exceedingly easy and quick. Beaks appear to have little more feeling than the nails on our fingers, except where they are joined. Perhaps you do not know it, but a bird's mandibles are composed of an inner skeleton base, and an outer, thin, horny case which fits on the bony part like your glove-finger upon your finger.

When I think of the uses birds put beaks or mandibles to I am astonished. They are awls, hammers, chisels, brushes, combs, trowels, and needles - yes! The Tailor-bird of India actually sews great leaves together in order to make a bag to hold its nest! They supply the place of hands. And do not some, like the Parrots, use them to climb with?

A study of beaks: Cormorant, Avocet and Spoonbill

What a variety of beaks we do see. The Eagle family, which includes the Hawks, Falcons, and Owls, have them powerful and curved, to cut and rend with. What is very providential too, is the splendid way in which Nature has given birds feet to correspond with their beaks. For instance, for an Eagle with a great curved bill to be provided with thin and comparatively weak legs and feet, say like a Curlew's, or Stork's, or a Snipe's, would be unwise, for it wants something to hold its prey while it tears it: and here the great strong sharp-clawed feet come in splendidly to help.

Now, if the Seagull had feet and toes like an Owl, what a muddle he would make of trying to swim: and the Owl would be equally badly off was he to have webbed feet like a Cormorant or a Puffin.

Now let us look at the seedeaters and crackers. These are mostly small birds. Our Fowls and Pheasants and Partridges might be termed seed or corn eaters. They do not rend or break, but pick up small particles of food. A hooked beak like a hawk's would be a great nuisance to them. The Goldfinch, Greenfinch, and even your Canary exhibit bills that snatch up seeds like a pair of tweezers, and being strong and sharp-edged, how easily do they split small seeds, to separate husk from the inside kernel. Rooks and Ravens, which grub about after larvae in hard soil, and often attack hard substances, have big conical mandibles. Birds that pry out small insects in bark-chink and crevice, and out of odd corners, have fine sharp bills, which are not nearly so robust as that of a Hawfinch, which has to crack cherry pips and hawthorn berries. Why, some birds, like Hedge sparrows, Flycatchers, and Tree Creepers, have them as sharp as needles. Birds that feed on caterpillars, moths, and flies, like the Cuckoo, the Swallow, and the Nightjar, have *soft* bills.

Then look at the birds which prowl on the ooze and mud and sand of our shores. With anything else but long bills many would perish. The Snipe bores deep down into the ditch-ooze for buried larvae and dormant insects. Curlews push down six inches to find the mud-worm and the tiny cockle. The Spoonbill, with its curious flat spoon-shaped mandibles, *spoons* the edges of broken mudflats to bring to light its prey.

A STUDY IN SPOONBILLS.

Spoonbills on Breydon

Chapter 17
SCRIBBLINGS OF A NATURALIST

"Life and summertime are all too short in this beautiful world of ours."

In 1911, Arthur wrote a series of chapters, twelve in all for another Primitive Methodist publication, *The Aldersgate Magazine*. *"By Leafy Ways"* was a favourite walk only a short train trip from home. It contrasts with the open marshland and Breydon, the subject of the next two chapters. One of his favourite companions on a nature ramble was Ben Dye, his baker-naturalist friend, who lost his sight in middle age.

By Leafy Ways

Two bits of tree-lined road - the one characterised by long stretches of red-trunked pines, the other by tall sweetbriar hedgerows, trend eastwards from St. Olave's Station.

St. Olave's Station
(courtesy of Eastern Daily Press)

Uniting the twain, like the bridge in a letter H, is one of the prettiest lanes in Suffolk. Three or four of us, old cronies, gossip and "dawdle" through Blokka Lane on as many summer afternoons as our numbers muster. It is but a four-mile ride from the bloater metropolis (Great Yarmouth); and within easy distance of it is the far-famed Fritton Decoy Lake, still noted for the netting of wild ducks. Over to the westward reaching from the blue Waveney to the reed-margined Yare, spread vast levels of marshes.

In the early summer the nightingale is busy with his family duties, finding time at less frequent intervals to make melody from the branches of a thick growing oak; occasionally showing himself to an admiring group of listeners sitting on the bluebell-dotted bank below. Yellow buntings dart hither and thither on business seriously bent; while a lark from an adjacent meadow warbles on fluttering wing above head, undisturbed by the fact that he may, a few months hence, be one of a ton and a half or tiny bird corpses bushelled out upon a game-stall with his little ones. The brisk sweet song recalls the verses of the poets, but the remembrance of last year's holocausts of "potted larks" checks each quotation that comes to mind.

The harsh laughing note of the green woodpecker is a familiar sound in the lane, and there is an aged tree, all too plainly splashed and marked by the rather dirty birds, with a round knothole doorway that advertises its nesting quarters. The next tree to it is a favourite with the squirrels by reason of its low-spreading branches, which afford convenient platforms for leaping from to others. One day my youngest son, Gerald, was leaning against this tree, quiet and motionless, when a bonnie little squirrel ran right up his back and leapt from his head to a handy horizontal, and was off with a lively scare on his hurriedly turning! The brown-jacketed rascals have sauced me more than once, "Chip! Chip! Chip!-ing to know what I wanted of them, bidding me take my departure.

There are five or six spots in Blokka Lane whereat my chums and I are delighted long to loiter. This is "Nightingale Rise", where the broom and the gorse hang out branches of bright yellow bloom, and the hawthorns spread a back grounding of white scented flowers. Here one of our numbers, a lover of birds and of solitude, whose sight has failed him (Ben Dye), loves to sit and bask in the sunlight and the sweet scents of the country. Poor Ben recounts incidents and observations on many a wild bird whose acquaintance he made in youthful days, for he, like an old man might, lives much in the past. Then there is the tiny one-plank footbridge that spans the "run" from the Decoy, which empties its surplus waters through leafy ways and crinkly "reaches" into the Waveney lower down. Its waters wash over much decaying vegetation that makes an unpleasant odour in the hotter days, notwithstanding the iris loves to hang out its yellow cravat above its speary leaves, and the woolly meadow-sweet diffuses a pleasant aroma.

Arthur with Ben Dye, the blind naturalist, in Blokka Lane

Blokka Lane at this point is guarded by tall willows and beeches, which make a pleasant dancing of lights, and shades as the summer winds bustle through their leafy tops and wave them to and fro. Life teems around; the bee winds his horn in a prolonged and sonorous cadence; burnet-moths flitter into view when disturbed by the winds; while tadpoles wag their fishlike tails in the running waters as they scuttle about and play and feed. Through the hedge we note the water-crowfoot spreading in swampy places in carpets of purest gold.

A little further on there is a "carr" where the pheasants wander down at times; stick-like alders and sallow start out from the boggy soil over which a soft moss spreads a covering of green. A narrow path zigzags through the carr and ends at the keeper's lodge. I slip down there on occasion to look at his gibbets - a clump of alders, whereon hang scores of badly-hunted, misunderstood stoats and weasels. Some are so mummified and decayed that they look like strips of leather, others are as fresh as if killed yesterday.

Hedgehogs of various sizes and periods hang around, while the foolish gamekeeper has also made sacrifices of kestrels and even owls - a farmer's unpaid friends". One day there may be seen a jay, and later on a magpie, and other "vermin". I think the fellow classes everything as vermin that does not claim to be honoured by the name of game. Hark!

> *"There's a blackbird and one or two thrushes,*
> *And a far-off wind that rushes,*
> *And the Cuckoo's sovereign cry*
> *Fills all the hollow of the sky!"*

These bonnie birds evidently hunt around by the gamekeeper's gallows, for the blowflies come too, and their ugly white larvae drop one by one into the grass below. The blackbird and the thrush are no doubt well aware of it; and thus the dead may feed the living!

My friends are by no means vandals, but they invariably leave Blokka Lane each with a handful of wild flowers for the vases at home, that they may for days to come recall sunlit hours in this little wild garden. The white hawthorn first yields up a spray of bloom, then the red campion and the ragged robin, the meadow-crowfoot and the iris bits of yellow, while the meadowsweet adds a touch of pleasant incense.

Later in the season other wild flowers show their pretty faces; while on the sandy upland which leads down to the marshes we always gather a bunch of purple heather. This is our last nosegay of the lessening year. With some of us it sees the winter through, often recalling pleasant hours when we strolled through leafy ways, and chats, discussions, and arguments on nature, art, and literary subjects, for all the "gang" are naturalists and philosophers - more or less.

Blokka Lane is one of my favourite walks, for among its trees I can almost always, in its season, make sure of the nightingale's song, no matter whether it be morning, noon or night. It was here that I first heard the drumming of the snipe and saw the fellow at his aerial performance.

What heated discussions there have been for decades as to how the snipe, at the time of nesting, booms his curious drumming. Some naturalists protested that this marvellous noise was a vocal effort - others as sagely and emphatically declared he made it by means of its wings. I heard a snipe drumming one early summer afternoon, and, presently, I espied him as I peered behind a tree in the lane. I had hidden myself so carefully, and was so silent, as a naturalist should be.

Snipe. Hard Times

"He who uses his eyes gets more fun out of a country walk than he who goes over the ground as if he were racing for a wager."

Chapter 18
AGAINST STONE CORNER

"Stone Corner, a little bay where the shore is entirely composed
of tiny spire shells."

In this imaginary winter walk along the north "wall" or embankment of
Breydon we are reminded of the plight of birds in winter. Stone Corner is
upstream of Duffells Rond, where Arthur's houseboat-observatory, the
"Moorhen", was propped up on stilts on the shore near Lockgate Farm.
Here Arthur had a base from which to watch birds and write.

A long devious "wall", a replica of the famous Dutchmens' dykes, surrounds
Breydon. But for it the marshy levels would be flooded at every tide. In
summer, wild birds would then again flock to what at once would become
saltings, to feed and to nest; and in winter the wildfowl would swarm there in
flocks and skeins. Today, as they have done for centuries, in the finer
months, fattening cattle revel in the semi-saline grasses. In winter they are
bare of sheep and cattle, and a dreary outlook is presented when snowflakes
whirl in the air and the rain beats pitilessly down.
Such are the outlooks one enjoys from Stone Corner. This "corner" is
nothing more than a sharp angle at a bend in the "walls," and juts out towards
the mudflats of the estuary imprisoned by the "dyke". It is here that the
prowling gunner hides when the wind is helpful, the tide rising, and winterly
weather is in the ascendant, waiting impatiently for passing duck and wader,
sometimes slaying or wounding a mallard, a wigeon, a curlew, or a grey
plover. His retriever, as alert and eager as himself, is ready at heel to do his
master's bidding, to plunge into the rough waters or to crash through the thin
ice in endeavour to capture or to seize the victim - alive or dead, as the case
may be.
Accompany me on a rimy morning in January, when Nature has "scattered
the hoar frost like ashes". It is slippery walking along the bank, which is
simply the wall-top. The grassy stubble crisply brushes our feet. Not a breath
of wind rustles among the dead reeds that stand out yellow and gaunt and
touched here and there with a sprinkling of frost and the remnants of a recent
snowfall. The ditch at the foot of the walls, dividing it from the marshes, is
hard frozen. The silence is broken by the voice of merry skaters on a distant
ditch or the melancholy wailing of some wild bird. On the white surface of
the ice are plainly marked the footprints of a meadow-pipit. The little fellow
has been eagerly hunting for some belated insect. Those larger markings are
the imprints of an almost equally hungry lark. The latter has not fared quite
so hardly, for he has been snapping off here and there a brittle grass-bent. He

manages fairly well in adverse days, for are there not still the cabbage patches on the outskirts of the town, where succulent leaves may be surreptitiously pecked at in the gardener's absence.

There are other signs that interest us. Those dotted imprints accompanying the footmarks of the birds, with the shoreline drawn here and there between them, suggest the progress of a rat that had been hard upon the trail of lark and meadow-pipit. Then some spaniel made larger footmarks that, out with his master, had suddenly forgotten the question of wildfowl, and, scenting the nearer game, had started upon the rat's well-defined track. Both trails end at a hole in the bank into which the rat had bolted for shelter. There are other "signs". On the wall at our feet lie some broken mussel shells. Some hooded crow had discovered these molluscs beside a tiny creek that was still trickling at the edge of a mudflat following the retreat of the ebb tide. He had brought the mussels one by one to the walls, having wrenched them from their attachments to a flint-stone. With vigorous onslaught he had smashed the shells with his hard mandibles and breakfasted luxuriously. The shellfish were a welcome change from the carrion he usually feasted upon.

Hooded crow and carrion

There is a gnarled stile at Stone Corner - a divide between adjacent properties. There, in days gone by, when wildfowl were more numerous, many a gunner had rested, and, on sight of likely prey, had crouched in hiding. At the foot of Stone Corner, below the sloping, sea-wrack-decorated

100

flints, which guard the front of the more friable clay in the creek, the punt-gunners squatted; for fowl will lead round a bend, as they follow the stream. Many a wigeon, mallard, teal, pochard and Scaup duck fell only half-a-century since in this neighbourhood on rare arctic days to the deadly belching of the punt-guns, which vomited forth a pound of leaden hail at a time. Today the birds are scarcer, the marshes, now that they are well drained, afford them so little inducement to frequent the neighbourhood. The old estuary itself has undergone corresponding changes. Nevertheless today, when very severe weather obtains, considerable flocks of wading birds - curlews, plovers, dunlins, and ducks, are found upon the muds and in the creeks, and, when the rising tide covers the mudflats, there comes after them a prowling gunner who has furbished and cleaned his aged fowling piece in anticipation of a slaughter. When the Broads are frozen over, the coots are driven hither in hundreds. They are quite eager to feed upon the "wrack" - the *Zostera marina* - a semi-marine water grass. And until they learn wit and become shyer, the gunners will secure many of them. Coots are not bad eating; and so for the prospect of a little gain men will dare ice and storm in their flat-bottomed punts and come hither to enjoy the excitement of the chase.

Leaning on the lichen-sprinkled stile we peer across the mudflats as far as the rime frost's chilly curtain will allow us. The sun, like a huge disc of Naples yellow, seems to be trying to pierce the mist. He looks dully bright as one seems him through smoked glass. An occasional crackling of the ice, the weird cry of a bewildered plover, and the distant crack of a gun, break the stillness and leave us guessing. We wonder what fell to that sharp retort. Maybe it was a coot, a wigeon, or a tufted duck. The gulls crackle fretfully now and then. They are hard put to it. Their vision is limited over the tidal waters beyond our own. The black-headed gull resorts to these flats, which the tide has bared, in search of mud-worms - the small red N*ereis diversicolor.* The herring gulls and black-headed gulls are glad to dine off the carcase of a stranded dog or cat, and are not slow to devour odd dead mice or rats washed up from the town, and even to glean up here and there a small shore bird that has escaped the gunner with broken wing and then died of its wounds.

There lies before us on the ice the suggestion of another tragedy. A few feathers, a spot or two of red blood, and leading up to them the footprints of a hooded crow. It is easy to re-enact the episode in one's mind. A wounded knot had fluttered beyond the reach of the gunner, and had fallen there to die. Its life-blood dyed the ice on which it lay. A hooded crow seeking a breakfast had espied the poor victim as he scouted around. You can see the spot where he alighted and then walked up to the dead bird. A confused trampling suggests how he set to work and tore to pieces the wader. Most of the feathers danced away on the breeze. A few flight feathers and a part of the legs remain. Head and bones are gone. Maybe some other crow came up to share the spoil, and the first-comer, snatching up the remains, flew to some safer spot to end his meal in selfish peace. Such are the little tragedies and dramas in bird life that can be read as well as sometimes seen at Stone Corner.

The sun at last breaks through the frosty atmosphere, and we see more clearly as the mist dissolves. Before us lies the old estuary with its flats and creeks, open and bare where the tides are busy, and blotched with white where the retreating waters left the ice stranded. Nearer to us small rafts of ice are jostling each other as they twirl in eddy, and swing round from an impact with the flat-edges or with other rafts. Nearer the main channel is a louder commotion as ice floes grate against each other, sometimes up-ending, and now and again pushing another as if possessed of a spirit of mischief. And so down to the sea they go.

A poor little dabchick in a pool yonder disconsolately hunts for a little fish. A bunch of dunlins, hard-pressed, seek mud-worms at the edge of a flat. They have to probe deep and often to find one. Gulls wheel around snatching up now and then some fragment they have espied between the ice floes, and out yonder in a creek a parcel of tufted ducks are snatching a short slumber even in the midst of Nature's turmoil.

A wintry walk to Stone Corner is not altogether uninteresting, when

> *"Gleamed the red sun athwart the wintry haze*
> *Which veiled the cold earth from its loving gaze.*
> *Nor to its cheerless beauty wert thou blind;*
> *To the keen eye of thy poetic mind*
> *Beauty still lives, though Nature's flow'rets die,*
> *And wintry sunsets fade along the sky!*
> *And nought escaped thee as we strolled along,*
> *Nor changeful ray, nor bird's faint chirping song."*

Chapter 19
A MARSHLAND POOL

"I love the level marshes and the lure of the muddy flats."

The moor and the mountains have no loud voices calling me to them: a Scotsman by descent, and a son of the marshes by birth, the vast low levels of East Anglia have ever had charms for me that have been irresistible. The lonely swamp, the interminable reed beds of the Broadlands, the level stretches of the cattle-dotted marshes, and even the mudflats of the estuary possess enchantments for me that beggar language. It may be something in boyish environments and early associations magnify these allurements. I am happy to be alone - if alone - with God and nature.

I call to mind one tiny pool, at a corner of a marsh, where I have spent hours in cogitating, and in watching the little tenants of its brackish waters, the callers on feathery wing, and frittering insects, which had attractions thither. Tall reeds, in spite of the slight percentage of saline flavouring, grew thickly at one end; sturdy irises or flags dotted their forefront with yellow ensigns in their season, whilst marsh mint and forget-met-nots and water plantains peeped out here and there. Tufts of sedge, and dainty rushes bending their brown tufted heads to the autumn winds, added a pleasing variety to the characteristic flora, while the bright eyes of *Glaux maritima* peered up at you from among the thick-growing marsh grasses around like dainty flowers in a richly coloured carpet.

Kingfisher. "Where innocence is bliss"

Among the rank-growing water weeds there was life abounding: minute creatures that the naked eye could not discover; the microscopical enthusiast found curious *Rotifera*; the entomologist netted in the weeds that cast shadows on the brown waters many rare *Microlepidoptera* and *Diptera* with strangely unpronounceable names. Larger and larger became the fellow tenants of the more minute forms, until the observer easily noted the gyrations of water beetles, the side-long scurrying of the "shrimps", notably *Gammarus Daubenii*, and the armadillo-looking *Sphoeroma rugicauda* pushing itself along by its linear-oval tail appendages, like tiny propellers, and now and again clasping some slender weed-stem, as one might grasp a straw in one's hand, shutting itself so roundly as to resemble a tiny bead upon a thread.   There on a muddy margin one saw the queer *Corophium* dragging itself along behind its unwieldy antennae. This fellow swims well, and does not descend, when outside its favourite element, to wriggle on its side like a *Gammarus*.

The naturalist is by no means the only creature interested in the life of a marsh pool, although most of these students of life in its varied forms go thither from selfish motives; the one may go for scientific interest; the others are actuated by less self-seeking promptings. Gnats and some other insects find in its waters a home for their future progeny; the majority call round for what they may pick up to bodily profit. Sandpipers - I've even see the ruff and reeve, the green sandpiper (*Tolanus ochropus*), the redshank, the wood sandpiper, the heron, and the mallard - all busily employed collecting sticklebacks, beetles, and most of the little beings whose queer names have already been mentioned.

 I one day saw a large dead flounder floating above the waterweeds. A heron had struck it on the muds of the adjacent estuary, had been disturbed, and not being able to swallow it, had flown hither to negotiate it, if possible, in peace. But his trying was vain, and after killing it, he had flung it away. In time the dead carcase floated, to the delectation of the "shrimps" and other carnivorous crustaceans. There are some small eels in the pool; how they came there is open to question: some one may have flung them therein when mere elvers; or a heron may have dropped them one by one. There lived herein for weeks a little shore crab, thrown in perhaps by an urchin. I saw that crab day after day scuttling in pursuit of any small creature settled on the mud within sight of him; sometimes he scrambled among the weeds after insects, or sticklebacks. If a water vole plunged in to swim to the other side, or to nibble a supper of luscious water-loving grasses, that crab speedily scuttled into hiding. I know that the water vole will tackle a dead or dying fish, but I question if the crab would have been sought after, although common brown rats will capture them with relish, for they bring shore crabs wholesale into my boat-house, and bite to pieces their hard shells for the sake of the juicy bodies that live inside these brittle skeletons. In search of water voles, the heron, in hard times, leaves the estuary and patiently watches at the entrances of their burrows, which open to the pool.

In autumn the nodding of the reeds and their whispers to the winds afford me great delight. Ah! How many times in my troubled youth did I not wander hither for the soothing of the music made by the wind as it rustled their long pointed leaves together? I pushed my way into the edge of the reed clump, and my spirit became attuned to the soft melody of their mellifluous dancing. There came only the lowing of the cattle, the crake of the landrail, the wail of the lapwing, and the chirping of the reed birds to break the rhythm, but adding to the harmony. That wild reed-bed was a means of grace to a jaded soul. There came colour in the glossy reed-tufts, in the metallic sheen of the blue and green dragonflies, and the dainty specklings of the various butterflies: indeed, there was seldom a want of colour, green predominating. The iris broke into patches of yellow; the forget-me-not dotted with a delicate blue; the cuckooflower paler still; later on the Michaelmas daisy hung out its brilliant purple stars. Before this the pink willow herb had bloomed, and the marsh thistle had hung out its stately blossoms.

Winter came along, pinching the remnant of vegetation that had not already succumbed to the maturing hand of autumn. The reed tufts turned white and woolly; the sedges and wild flowers had shrivelled and broken. The swallows that in summer hunted for insects around the pool had been replaced by the meadow-pipits, linnets, and hardier species. The mallard flew round only to find the waters turned to ice; and even the snipe, prying into the likeliest corners, sadly turned his back, and went off seeking running creeks, where moving waters kept open spaces, or saltier pools still defied the grip of winter: and

> *"The dead leaves strew the forest walk,*
> *And withered are the pale wild flowers:*
> *The frost hangs blackening on the stalk,*
> *The dewdrops fall in frozen showers."*

Looking back over the years there still come living pictures of this obscure pool to my mind's eye when memory takes me there again. One day there came a small fly to an opening wild flower, just to dip its tiny proboscis among the honey-laden petals. A hungry wasp struck at it and bore it to the top of a plantain leaf, where it killed it speedily, nipped off its gaudy wings, and bore away its dismembered body. A field vole venturing out for a late breakfast was promptly seized on by a kestrel, which flew to an overhanging rail, and there tore the little rodent to pieces for his own. A cuckoo, probably mistaken for a hawk, flew by mobbed by a parcel of perching birds; a heron was about to alight at the margin, when a slight movement on our part caught his keen eye, and with a wild discordant note he turned again and fled.

On another occasion the day was hot and oppressive. The cattle on the marshes heavily panted as they lay chewing the cud. I crept round a low bank that faced one side of the pool. A huge farm-horse stood there quietly dozing, his forefeet fetlock deep in the cool waters. Around him were eight redshanks, whose sealing wax-like legs looked unduly long by reflection; three lapwings, three blackheaded gulls, and three ringed plovers, the farthest being not more than six feet away from his hoofs. The redshanks were at their toilet; the pewits gossiping; and the bonnie ringed plovers pretending to find something to eat, and occasionally I think they managed to capture a "shrimp". The others were lazily looking on. And then on one piercing winter's day upon the ice that hid the waters lay a patch of blue. It was the carcase of a kingfisher by cold and hunger slain.

Chapter 20
BIRD-WATCHING IN A BREYDON PUNT

"The Birds around me hopped and played;
Their thoughts I cannot measure:
But the least motion which they made,
It seemed a thrill of pleasure."
-Wordsworth

In 1907 Arthur wrote chapters for *"The Book of the Open Air: British Country Life in Spring and Summer",* edited by Edward Thomas. Selected from them is a trip on Breydon in Arthur's punt.

The Patient Observer

The dew sparkles on every leaf bud and grass-blade, and the skylark sings merrily above head on a bright May morning. The sun has climbed his rosy way just high enough to tinge the ruddier hues of the pantiles of the quaint old houses on the opposite quayside, and to fling a glare of burning light on the freckled surface of the tide gliding by our boathouse doors. A few big sea slaters (*Ligia oceanica*) are sunning themselves on the woodwork, and a number of banded *Nemoralis* snails are loitering still to nibble at the succulent grasses topping the "wall"; while a parcel of black-headed gull, rejoicing in their nuptial hood and the glorious morning, are taking a few hours' respite from the cares of nesting, and seeking a change of diet from inland grub and earthworm: they dip at every edible morsel that floats on the tide - floating fish or struggling insect, and daintily drop toe-deep into the water as they snatch at some high-swimming *Idotea linearis*, or "sea-louse". How carelessly and merrily they scream!

It is but the matter of a few minutes getting our punt afloat, one foot as we push her scrunching a handful of broken carapaces and legs of hapless shore crabs that, last night, a couple of brown rats discussed at supper time: they hunt on the mud at low water, sometimes even by daylight, their footprints and tail-streaks dotting thickly here and there. Our gun-punt is a typical Norfolk boat, eighteen feet long, pointed at both ends, like a collier's pickaxe, broad amidships, and where the haft fits in is where the punter sits to row - in the "well" of the craft. She is flat-bottomed, drawing only three or four inches of water; she was built for a watcher of birds, and not a butcher. We can glide over the "flats" in shallows that a keeled boat dare not negotiate. Decked fore and aft, with a low rail round the "well", we care little for the wintry waves into which she dips her nose, for the broken water runs off at once from the slightly rounded deck. Today there is but the merest ripple; we won't ship the mast, for speed is unnecessary, and the lockers contain creature comforts. I will sit amidships and scull; you be seated on the stern and keep those binoculars handy.

The wind is fair from the southeast, a quarter beloved by every local wildfowler and ornithologist when the migrants are moving in spring or autumn. You heard the shrill pipings and the mellow whistling above head last night, which told you birds were on their travels, and had halted awhile to circle around and puzzle out the meaning of so many strange lights beneath them. The curlew "whauped", the grey plover "kle-a-ed", and the dunlin blew his key-like note in shrilly monosyllables. We hope to see some of them breakfasting on the flats.

We are overtaken as we near the great railway bridge which now spans the entrance to Breydon by a picturesque Norfolk wherry, whose deeply-laden hull, built on the selfsame lines as its early predecessors, the Vikings' ships, and huge sail, always befits a Broadland picture; a careless fellow, hands in pockets, leans against the winch on the forepeak, whistling a popular air, his mate smoking a fragment of clay pipe at the tiller cleverly manipulates sail and rudder. Other wherries ahead dot Breydon, and bending to the steady breeze, keep to the "channel", marked plainly enough by a four-mile row of red painted "stakes" on the left, and a row of black ones on the right. Far away on the skyline windmills, and here and there a marsh-man's cottage, show above and break the monotony of the "walls", while a half-dozen Breydoners' houseboats give spots of colouring below them. Above all is the blue, speckled here and there with a few swift-moving clouds of Naples yellow.

We pull up at the "Lumps" just inside the five-stake drain, putting to flight half-a-dozen town pigeons that have been gleaning among the drifted *Zostera* blades that the tide has flung up among the wiry rond-grass and stunted glasswort. Their quest for *Hydrobia ulvae*, split-pea-sized molluscs very like *Limnoea stagnalis* in shape. The pigeons fill their crops with them: we later on find every floating chip and every blade of *Zostera marina* dotted thickly with the species. A half-score loquacious whimbrels take to wing in an opposite direction: they have been pushing their scimitar-shaped bills into the holes of the mud-worms (*Nereis*) and picking up here and there a shrimp and *Gammarus*. How conspicuously the white of their hinder quarters shows up against the brown mud and between their grey, sharp, curved wings! The noisy "May-bird" of the old race of gunners was always greatly disliked, for it did sentry-go for flocks of friendly waders, and was always the first to warn of danger.

We purpose lying in a little creek for half-an-hour, by which time the flats, higher up, will be covered, and the birds driven from their feeding grounds must come this way for a foothold, or go to the marshes to nap or preen their feathers, and chat over plans for the morrow's doings. Already a couple of knots, unnoticing us crouching in the punt, and decoyed into halting by an imitation of their note, have alighted on the drift left at last night's high-water mark; and a trio of turnstones, clad in the black and white and ruddy brown of spring, with legs of orange-red, have joined them. Right merrily the turnstones commence to fling aside the wrack and bits of flotsam under which hide *Gammarus marinus* and many a shore-hopper, and which skip or wriggle to the right or left on being so unexpectedly exposed to view. They do not reap the benefit of all their labour, for the friendly knots do not mind sharing in the spoils, while a quartet of dunlins in their vests of black promptly step in and dodge and rob the turnstones with amusing impudence. Twice the turnstones in turn pretend to punish them with open bill, but their menaces are unheeded, and they repeat their pilfering at the earliest moment, and finally tire the patience of their larger friends, who with a low clear note take to wing and leave them.

Walking sedately on the far side of the lumps are several curlews, piping between their probings in that self-complacent trilling note which bespeaks contentment and satisfaction. How adroitly the long bill is thrust down to where the clams are hiding. It is amusing to see how the curlew timidly jumps aside as an equally startled mollusc squirts up its surplus water; but it is to its own undoing, for the bird immediately digs down, and if it is not too big hauls it out, and forthwith devours it. The curlew sometimes muds his "face", for the clam as often lies six inches buried, and the curlew usually has

Expectation. Turnstones and Ringed Plover

but a five and a half-inch bill with which to nab him! The shorecrab provides the curlew with many a breakfast, but he never profits by his failures to swallow any but the tiniest of flounders. Yet he can never refuse to toy with a fish he knows it is impossible for him to bag, and the wily gulls standing watchfully around know that there will be a chance for one of them when he flings it away in disgust.

Not fifty yards from where we are skulking, less than two years ago, I saw nine dainty avocets sitting afloat in this very drain, dancing up and down on the rippled waters just as you see a fleet of ships riding at anchor; and some of them, duck-like dipped with tails up, pricking their needle bills in the soft ooze for molluscs; and if perchance they discovered a mud-worm it suited them just as well. One of the delights attending a trip among the mudflats is the unremote possibility of falling in with unexpected rarities. I have thus come across an Iceland gull, a stork, a Caspian tern, and a pelican asleep with his pouch full of flounders, and many a spoonbill. And only quite recently a friend of mine saw four glossy ibises; he went next day to try and get a shot at them, and fell in with thirteen red crested whistling ducks instead, and with punt and shoulder gun secured nine!

Arthur and friend, Arthur H Smith, tied up to the wreck "Agnes" on Breydon

Let's make now for the "Ship" drain. But stay! turn your glasses on yonder herons near the "walls"; they are fishing for eels and flounders in the North Wall drain. You will observe that they are in the excellent plumage of springtime, their long glossy black crests waving in the wind, like pennants. You will notice, too, that they do not stand still and wait, Micawber-like, for what may turn up, as juvenile herons do; but like grotesque sentries they march along by the edge of the flat and snatch up victims that would evade them. Young birds exhibit more patience, no doubt, but exercise less commonsense.

Those two rows of short, scraggy, upright timbers are all that is left to view of the old brig, *Agnes*. Let us fasten the punt to a couple of them: this is a favourite post of observation of mine. The *Agnes* regularly crawled to the Straits and back in the days of Nelson, carrying wine and fruit; they knew stem from stern by the jutting out bowsprit. In the 1870s the Commissioners (Port and Haven) brought her and sunk her here at the mouth of a drain: there was far too much scouring taking place under the protecting wall, by all the body of water that dropped off the flats at the ebb tide. They cut the drain with a more circular sweep into the Channel. In 1878 a pair of swallows nested under her decks notwithstanding the hold was then always full of water; today where the decks were is hard mud, dry save at high water. The resting gulls delight on sunny days to roost on top of these oaken ribs and dry their spotless plumage after meals and bath, and sleep there until hungry again - or disturbed by the likes of us. Our glasses sweep the whole of Breydon. Several black terns on their way to their breeding quarters trip gaily along, nimble as swifts, and quite as erratic in their flight, now poising themselves aloft, anon dipping without apparent effort, until they plunge their mandibles in the water as they fasten upon some floating insect. Today is hardly a black terns' day, for they are more often seen here on a rougher breeze, when they exhibit the liveliest movements. They come to Breydon from the southeast, and will only stop but to fish as they proceed, and pass on out at the northeast corner, to show themselves in an hour or so at Hickling Broad or Horsey Mere. They used to breed at Upton, near Acle; you can see Acle Church from here through my favourite 8 x Zeiss's.

Whimbrel

Hardly so actively, yet with spirited dash, yon little terns are fishing in the drain; what they are catching it is hard to say; when they come back in August with their squealing youngsters they will revel in an abundance of herring-syle that sport in myriads just beneath the surface. It is interesting to watch them, heads down, dashing to and fro, now hovering like kestrels, now plunging with the earnestness of gannets, but without the power to submerge themselves. More curlew and herons are fishing in the Ham in front of us, the latter thigh deep, and persistent; the curlews restlessly, and with apparent impatience at the rising of the tide. The noisiest bird, next to the whimbrel, is the ringed plover; he never takes to wing but he hints to his friends that they had better be moving also. Fully fifty now went by in whirring flight, several grey plovers passing with them. The "greys" drop down on the flat behind us, and at half a leg's length find bottom. See how they have drawn up a leg and stuck their bills into their shoulders, and have fallen asleep in an instant. One pulls his beak out and straightens his neck at our imitation of his call-note, but he is so tired he makes no reply, and drops to sleep again. You will observe what black vests they wear, and how the neck of it comes up quite to their eyes, its intensity of colour throwing the mottled back into high relief. The bird always calls to mind a pet ratel (honey-badger) whose fur was lighter above than below. The golden plover does not often visit us in spring, nor does he show such a spread of black; but how much they are alike in winter. You need make no mistake in springtime when you hear the grey plover calling "*Kle-a-ee,*" and the golden answering "*tirr-pe-u!*" nor need you in winter, if you will remember that the grey has a small hind toe, while his cousin has not.

A hundred dunlins dash by, making for the "Lumps"; a score of ringed plovers join them. A common tern and a curlew-sandpiper flit past the moment after. We recognise the "stint-like pigmy" by its conspicuously white rump, and by its less shrill, longer-drawn, key-whistled note. We haven't observed a godwit today, but we have heard its silvery "*lou-ee*". It is rarely that a few bar-tailed godwits forget to put in an appearance in the middle of May: prior to the 1870s its flocks were regularly looked for; half a century ago great quantities were recorded and the gunners called the 12th of May "Godwit Day." I have seen seventy in a day before now, but not lately. Why they have forsaken us is hard to say: Breydon remains, and protection is assured, although the condition of the flats has considerably altered. It cannot, however, be a lack of food, or why do the whimbrel come in equal, if not in increasing numbers? And we see the spoonbill much more frequently.

Heighho! Look yonder in the direction of Rotten Eye: that white stately upstanding object *is* a spoonbill. We are in luck's way today. A host of inquisitive gulls surround him as he sweeps his big flat mandibles in successive half-circles on the ooze below; he is searching for worms and molluscs, and sifts them under water as shrimpers riddle their shrimps, to wash away what is useless - the mud. He stops now and again to try and negotiate a flounder, misjudging his capacity for swallowing, and finally flings away the lifeless thing, which is eagerly snapped up by the attendant

Twelfth of May – "Godwit-Day"

*Black-tailed Godwit and Greenshank. Arthur named his punt
"Yarwhelp", the local name for Godwit*

gulls.   Rarely they are impudent, and worry "spoonie", or "banjo-bill", as we call him, but in time they come to tolerate the silent, harmless fellow, who, in return, repays their forbearance by choosing to sleep in their midst, for he soon learns that they are not silent when danger threatens, and even the patter of their feet as they run to gain an impetus for flight, quickly awakes him. He unquestioningly joins them in their flight, and finds out the reason as he hastens with them to a safer spot.

Arthur, sailing his Breydon punt to his houseboat-observatory, The Moorhen

We have arrived at the *Moorhen*, our old Noah's ark, perched high and dry and shored up on Banham's rond, by Lockgate Farm. She used to bear her owner in her smarter days into Broadland haunts; her present moorings, like the old ship *Agnes's* are final. She is now our "observatory". Tie the punt to the little jetty, and step inside. Fold up those blankets, and set the table from this cupboard, while I light a fire and put the kettle on. While the water boils we'll sit in the stern sheets outside. The tide is at its full, and will presently begin to ebb. On the rond to the right are a score and more curlews waiting its fall. Some redshanks from the marshes impatiently hurry by, and, like Noah's dove, return, to come again shortly when there is standing room assured. A greenshank flits by just after, uttering his loud clear "*pleu! pleu! pleu!*" We heard him piping a mile away. He settles in a "low" in the rond, and immediately begins to methodically work the shallow puddle. Away to the right a mile or more, on the "Fleet" near Dan Banham's Mill, a hundred black specks dot the waters. Take this old telescope, and see if you recognise them. They are wigeon. Most of them appear to be asleep; one now and again may be observed tugging at the *Zostera* - the "wigeon grass" of the old gunners - waving beneath it; this bird delights to feed on the succulent stems of this semi-marine species of vegetation, and most adroitly nips off the less palatable blades of darker green, which float downstream on the ebb tide to tell some ancient eel-babber that the "smee" have been dining in goodly numbers "up above", and he sighs (if these passionless men ever do) when he remembers how he, in the old days, *"afore protection done for him"*, used to *"cut lanes"* through their ranks with his swivel gun. The coffee is ready; and the sandwiches invite discussion.

A flock of large gulls is gathering a hundred yards or more away in front of us. There are at least fifteen adult great black-backed gulls, and twenty of a younger generation, clad in the mottled grey of the second year; two others are blotched, and have already passed their third year. Myriads of shore-crabs prowl about among the *Zostera*, chasing each other in anger when not pursuing shrimps and gobies, and running after each other again in envious mood when one has secured its prey. On these greedy crustaceans the gulls are feeding. With sometimes four thousand gulls on Breydon, it is a wonder to me that any crabs remain at all!

The tide is falling fast. Back to the flats come the curlews, and the redshanks, and the smaller waders from the marshes, knowing the times of rise and fall as if they worked by tide-table. All the waders seem hungry again. The whimbrel are leaving the rond and joining the curlews. Small gulls, wearied of their fishing in the Channel, make for the bare mud patches to rest awhile. The herons have gone back with their catches to their nesting quarters at Reedham. We quant across Breydon, following a sinuous drain that forms a sort of tributary to the river-like Duffell's Drain, which cuts Breydon diagonally almost exactly in two. The upper portion of Breydon we have not had time to explore today. At the entrance of Duffell's Drain, where it joins the main Channel, lies moored the watcher's houseboat, to which we make fast for half-an-hour's gossip, and to compare notes. We need not hurry, for it is an easy half-hour's pull downstream to our boatshed.

Arthur's houseboat, Moorhen, at Lockgate Farm, on the north wall of Breydon

Chapter 21
A MINUTE AND A HALF WITH "JOHN KNOWLITTLE"

Arthur contributed to many local company's journals; this is a page from *The Carrow Works Magazine*, January 1920, written for Colman's employees by F. R. Widdows.

"Could you spare me a minute and a quarter, Mr Patterson?"

"Well, I'll make it a minute and a half," came the cheery reply - and Mr Arthur H. Patterson, known far and wide as "John Knowlittle", the talented and entertaining Norfolk Naturalist, assisted me from my invalid chair and conducted me to his "den".

"There," was the remark as he deposited me very tenderly in a most desirable armchair, "now you are in a chair that was given to me by Her Grace the Duchess of Bedford, I hope you are comfortable." I assured him that I felt not only comfortable but honoured, and perfectly at home, and was proceeding to apologise for taking up his valuable time when he broke in with -

"Now don't mention it; I have just an hour at my disposal, and I am only too pleased to have a chat. My den is a bit in disorder - although that's not unusual - but we can talk for all that. What did you say? Oh, yes, of course. *"Through Broadland in a Breydon Punt"*. I am glad you liked the articles in the *Eastern Daily Press;* look I'm just getting them into book form. And here is the awning that sheltered me; just two coats of dressing, that's all, and in good order now, isn't it?" Then from a recess he drew an empty kit bag, that told its own sad story of a young and promising life surrendered for King and Country (his youngest son, Gerald); while the escaping sign was all too plainly charged with the same deep sorrow expressed by King Solomon, when he cried, "O my son Absalom! O Absalom, my son, my son!"

The den was certainly an ideal sanctum for a naturalist. It contained two fine book cases running over with books by the best authors, sketches and photographs of birds and animals, manuscripts galore and various natural history specimens, including the latest addition, a magnificent pair of horns of the hartbeest, one of the graceful antelopes of South Africa. "And," said Mr. Patterson in a sort of confidential aside as he brought the last-mentioned before me, "I'm not at all certain whether the Norwich Museum can show a pair like 'em". Without the slightest restraint he talked away, giving me incident after incident connected with his long and eventful life as a naturalist, until my consciences began to prick me on the matter of time, and I expressed the fear that my "minute and a half" must be drawing to a close.

118

"Oh, never mind that, don't go for a minute; here, let me do you a sketch to take away. What shall it be? Ah, that will do, I'll give you a portrait of myself, or as much of myself as I can remember." And in the caper of a broomstick - if I am to use that term to express rapidity of movement - I was in possession of "The Mudlark of Breydon".

"The Mudlark" on Breydon - a self-caricature

Pencil and India rubber have neither part nor lot with Mr. Patterson's sketches. The pen is in the ink, the ink has assumed shape on the paper, and the sketch is finished in less time that it would take an ordinary mortal to outline his subject.

"This is far more than I expected, Mr. Patterson, and I fear I've nothing to give you in return."

"Not a word, my dear sir, Norwich people are so very kind to me, and take so much interest in my work, that they occupy a very warm place in my heart, and I'm only too happy to please them in any way I can. They are always ready to encourage and help me. Now let me sketch a bird for you" - and "PRESTO" sketch number two was in my pocket book.

We talked on, and I discovered, very easily, that any information bearing either upon fauna or flora was acceptable to Mr. Patterson. A reference to

119

wild animals led me to tell him I twice took it into my head to conduct a Sunday afternoon service in a Menagerie for the benefit of the keepers, attendants, human freaks and the like. My text, "A living dog is better than a dead lion," made him exclaim, "Capital!" and his kindly eyes twinkled with amusement when I described the unsuccessful efforts of a den of lions and a cage of chattering monkeys to talk me down, albeit I was so, for a brief space at the commencement of my address, to give way to the lions."

"I should like to sit here and continue our chat for a year, Mr. Patterson."

"And I dare say I could find up a few stories to interest you if you did; but although our meeting must now come to an end, let me say that I shall always be pleased to see you, and, further, I shall be ready and willing to write a short article on some natural history subject for the *Carrow Works Magazine* whenever it may be desired."

"A very kind offer, Mr. Patterson, and, on behalf of the Editors of the C.W.M., I thank you most warmly. I will take the responsibility of promising that a copy of the Magazine shall be sent to you each quarter".

With his assistance I rose from the chair presented by Her Grace the Duchess, and prepared to take my leave.

"By the way, Mr. Patterson, what is your correct Yarmouth address?"

"Well, I can't put my hand on a visiting card for the moment, but this will serve the purpose" - and he handed me – a compliments form.

A. H. PATTERSON,
Naturalist.
Ibis House,
Gt. Yarmouth.

with
"John Knowlittle's"
Compliments

A H Patterson 1919

120

Chapter 22
AN IDEAL RIVER TRIP

"The Victorious" claimed to be the only pleasure steamer embarking from the Southtown side of Yarmouth Bridge. She was a very comfortable boat, with ample saloon accommodation and convenience. Refreshment of all kinds could be obtained on board, Lemon and Dash, Lime Fruit, Lemonade, Claret and Lemon, Stone Ginger Beer, Dry Ginger Ale, all manufactured by Lawrance's, were some of the beverages on offer to the voyager. The excursion gave the visitor *"the unique opportunity to combine a Broadland river trip with the pleasure of spending three hours in a sylvan retreat of exquisite beauty".* Known as "The Switzerland of Norfolk", the Brundall pleasure gardens were popular and to further increase the enjoyment for the visitor, the owners, The Brundall Gardens Steamship Company Limited, commissioned Arthur to write a guide. He described the run up from Berney Arms:

The marsh grasses are rank and fattening; hence the thousands of cattle turned out for the summer months. Each marshman (who usually tends one or two miles) walks miles daily, seeing to the cattle; often has he to fetch rope and blocks to haul one out of a ditch.

Marshland Cattle

A noisy, excitable bird, on sharp white pinions, with red legs, nests on the marshes. It whistles a shrill "clu clu clu". It is the redshank. Often our boat puts up some small twittering birds from the mud of the riverbanks - they're sandpipers. Herons fly up, and pass in lumbering flight overhead; they are after flounders, water voles, eels, or shrimps. The mills contain scores of swallows' nests, which are built on spikes, or in crumbled brick holes. The salt air of Breydon has provoked a healthy thirst. Let's go in the cabin, and have a cup o' tea, a bottle of "pop", or something stronger.

You will notice, inside the river walls, stretches of level grassy "ronds"; these are part of the original marshes that are cut through by the "walls". This is a wild bit of broadland until we reach Reedham, where a charming riverside village woos the eye. Just before reaching the railway swing bridge you will observe a straight canal; that runs to St. Olaves on the Waveney. A wherry sailing from Norwich to Lowestoft saves several miles by using it.

The Norfolk and Suffolk wherries which sail by are graceful vessels, almost flat-bottomed, carrying 30 to 40 tons. The huge sail is usually worked by one man, who guides the tiller by his hips. Sometimes wife and kiddie live with Dad in the small cabin astern. The wherry is a survival of the Vikings' sea boats. The long pole used in a bad "reach" is called a quant - quaint, isn't it? With the head against his shoulder he may have to shove a mile or more at a bad bend. Most are glad to rest near the few-and-far-between hotels!

Norfolk Wherries

Legend tells us that in A.D.870, one Lodbrog, a Dane, who had been hawking (with birds, of course), was driven by a storm, and landed on the "cliffs" at Reedham. King Edmund (then camping there) received him graciously. Berne, the King's huntsman, grew jealous, and slew Lodbrog. The angry King set Berne adrift, and he landed in Denmark, and told lies. In a great rage Hinguer and Hulba came with 20,000 Danish men, executed innocent Edmund, and soon ravished all East Anglia. I have found Reedhamites are hospitable to this day.

Reeds, river-bends, mills, marsh farms, swallows and yachts all the way, make pictures without end. In Autumn the riversides are gay with Michaelmas daisies *(Aster maritima)*. At "Haysel" (hay-making) there is more life in the scene, and a delightful aroma. Here and there are seen fishing boats "stowed" until the autumn herring fishing calls them. Two idling ships look much out of place here. At Reedham is seen the first of the ferryboats - huge floating pontoons that carry horses, cattle, and motorcars slowly and "clanketty" across the river. We pass the "Cockatrice", where many a strange marsh tale has been told, and in years again many a smuggler halted there. The real "Cockatrice" may have been a sort of viper - something that stung, like the scorpion, or the cobra. Close by is Hardley Cross - a stone that marks the respective boundaries of the Norwich and Yarmouth jurisdictions over the river. At one time an annual "pow-wow" was held by the members of the said combination - a sort of beating the bounds with "a riot of bell and speech".

We are now in a neighbourhood, which delights anglers, who catch big bream.

Cantley comes next with its tall chimneys, a landmark for miles, and sugar manufactory, a busy spot when trainloads of sugar beets are piled into a veritable mountain. If farmers were sufficiently wise, they'd grow enough to make the mill work all the year round. Here is a favourite resort for yacht-sailing matches.

Moorhens often flutter from side to side, trailing their feet through a bubbling pathway; swans too, with their dusky youngsters, are interesting features. Every year the young swans are caught and "upped", that is marked on the bills with their owner's insignia.

Brundall comes into view soon after passing Buckenham Ferry. There is a fine array of houseboats along the last two reaches - boats of every size and design; some large enough to make comfortable diggings, even in winter. The trees, which have been rising into notice ever since we left Cantley, now begin to make the scenery exceedingly picturesque; and the white sails of passing yachts show off to advantage the delightful tints of varying foliage.

Every bend adds to the glorious panorama. We catch glimpses of Surlingham Broad.

Here we are at last at our resting place, near by the huge, smart Tea Room, where a couple of hundred persons may sit down to lunch; and later, when the place is cleared, dance many waltzes on the beautiful floor. Here too, near by, is the spanking new and inviting "Riverside Hotel", where every sort of refreshment, bar spirituous appearances, may be looked for. From thence the visitor takes the trail to the Gardens - and such gardens. What a wealth of oaks, weeping ashes, and elms, and coniferous trees of many sorts, all so lovingly planted by the dear old Doctor Kimberley, who spent a small fortune upon its beautification. What walks, glades, arbours and leafy nooks lead up from the lily-smothered lake to the hilltop, where miles of landscape hold the onlooker enraptured?

Hid in a wild corner is a queer stone animal, called the Roebuck.

I hardly like the name of Brundall Gardens. It is a slice of woodland borrowed from Eden. For once (if not more) our visitors should come to see it, if only for the glorious "voyage" up and down stream. You leave Yarmouth at 10; get here by 12.30: walk the woodlands, or visit the clean and pretty village: "dawdle" around, and refresh yourself until 4. At 6.30 you may ask your Yarmouth landlady to set "high tea" at your apartments. After tea, there are the Piers and Bands and Cinemas making you vastly welcome.

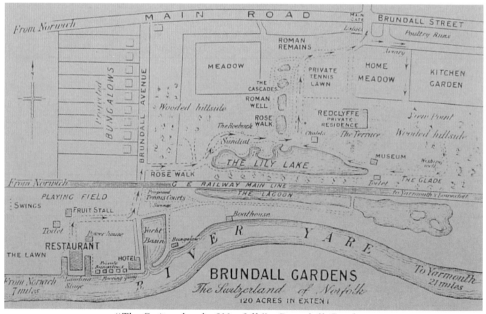

"The Switzerland of Norfolk" - Brundall Gardens

Chapter 23
JOHN KNOWLITTLE'S SWAN SUPPER

"Old Breydoners' Reminiscence at Yarmouth."

Menu card

The fourth and the last Swan Supper took place on January 27th, 1934; the following report appeared in the *Eastern Evening News* the next day:

At the bidding of Mr. A.H. Patterson ("John Knowlittle") there assembled at Johnson's Rooms, Yarmouth, several Breydon wildfowlers and naturalists to enjoy a swan supper and gossip over old times.
This was the fourth meeting of its kind to take place in the past thirty years. Each muster has revealed the passing of many of the "old crew", and now there were few indeed. Those present included Messrs. Walter Brand, Tom Clements, E.A. (Ted) Ellis, Harry E. Hurrell, Arthur Patterson, his son John Patterson, Jack Quinton, Philip Rumbelow, Lee Spink, the brothers Sharman and friend, Westgate, and

125

Wigg. The host had prepared menu cards decorated with sketches, humorous and otherwise, of birds.

Dr. Lee Spink proposed the loyal toast and one to the memory of old Breydoners. He referred to the precarious living these men had snatched from the estuary. They had been with nature, he said, observant, with retentive memories, and were able to recount incidents in a way that was vivid, clear, and truthful, adding much to our knowledge of birds. They could no longer obtain a livelihood in the old way, and but one or two were left who had done so.

Mr. Jack Quinton, aged 81, replied to the toast, and recalled the old days. In the 1860s he was using a gun that carried a pound of shot. When the first watcher (Ducker Chambers) was installed in the close season they "didn't care a button" for him. He always purchased the Bird Protection Acts as they came out, and learned them by heart. In this way he was able to confuse the old-fashioned sergeants when accosted. He had tramped the marshes, shot round all the broads from Hickling eastward and had lived on ruffs and reeves for a fortnight.

Mr. H. Hurrell (manager of the Eastern Daily Press office in Regent Street) proposed the "Health of Mr. Patterson", who, he said, missed nothing of the glory of nature on the day's march.

Mr. P. Rumbelow (a fellow naturalist) replied on Mr. Patterson's behalf. He said there was always a difficulty in distributing local natural history records between Norfolk and Suffolk. This applied to Breydon: and Mr. Patterson must often wish that Lothingland was not "over the border." Stuffed birds were now of no value - a matter for congratulation.

Mr. Quinton (a bird-catcher) then related the history of the bird in question, working up to the point when "Hoppy" Smith, the taxidermist, refused £320 for it offered him by Lord Lilford. Eventually it was sold to Chase of Birmingham for £17, and Smith did not get all of this. At the same time he was offered £5 for Lilford's historic letter, but he still tried to bargain, and in the end burnt it as he was dying.

Mr. W. Brand followed with Breydon memories - recalling "Mussle", "Pintle", "Gabey", and "Gut" Thomas, "Silky" Watson, "Fiddler" Goodens, Pero Pestell and his perpetual longing for a "bit o' bacca", Jimmy Hurr, the Thackers, Sharmans, and "Admiral" Gooch. He described the jealous code of the fraternity. A newcomer was welcomed very slowly, and given his position for gunning or (eel) picking. One incurred enmity and reprisal when he encroached on another's preserve - and he would be kept "on the books" a twelvemonth, and get little sport during that time.

Mr. Quinton remembered an occasion when 27 big-gun shots were expended on less than seven ducks that continually "dove (dived) to the flash".

So the stories went on round the fire till late into the evening. There may never be another Breydoners' Swan Supper.

Chapter 24
THE JOYS OF A NATURALIST

*"How I love nature even to her minutest details – how in quite a different
world I seem when I get away from the busy, whirling haunts and
ways of men, and lose myself in admiring and mixing and drinking
in the delights of nature clear away from them."*

When wanting a change from the open mudflats and Yarmouth rivers,
Arthur enjoyed a nature ramble on the sandy heathland at Belton, reached
by a short trip on the train from Southtown Station, Great Yarmouth.   In the
early days, often Ben Dye, the blind naturalist, accompanied him, but on a
summer day in 1927 his companion was the young Ted Ellis. Arthur enjoyed
the company of Ted, a Guernsey boy whose family had moved to
Gorleston.   His passion for nature study reminded Arthur of that of his own
son, Gerald, so tragically taken from him in 1916.   He encouraged Ted to
record and write about his observations, and became his mentor.
Arthur recorded some words by a Dr. Harvey:

"The true naturalist is always ready to share his pleasure with others, and
only half enjoys what he cannot share."

Ted visited Arthur at his houseboat "The Moorhen" on many occasions. A
hasty letter might be written saying, "I shall be up at the boathouse at Acle -
bring a sleeping bag…" Ted, undoubtedly, filled a gap in the old man's life.
An article in the *Eastern Daily Press* in August 1927 records an excursion
by Arthur and Ted Ellis to Tom Brookes' "little bit of Suffolk fen" at Belton.
Today much of the sandy heathland has been built over, but in his day it
was a naturalist's paradise.

Naturalists are born optimists; only the worst of a microscopical hobby
means a concentrated fiddling-about in the open; isolation, exclusiveness and
more concentration in the laboratory, hence so few have the keenness to
tackle it and the patience.
Now, give me a roving, mooching commission and tangible objects, and I am
there, my only paraphernalia a pair of binoculars, an old *E.D.P.* for wrapping,
a bit of string and penknife and a lens, some Marching Chocolate (Caley's), a
stick and a few tin matchboxes, and a fine - No, any old sort of day is the
same to me. And if the way is long, a country pub in view, in whose hard-
seated parlour I may sit with William Hazlitt - he to read his *"New Eloise"*
over a bottle of sherry, and a cold chicken - I with my pot of tea, a hunk of
bread and cheese and with mine host and a fairly intelligent old mole-catcher
from the stubbles.

THE BAIT THAT DRAWS

Advertisement by Arthur Patterson for CALEY'S Marching Chocolate

On Tuesday I trained to Haddiscoe, walked thence to Fritton Lake, and with young Ellis, who has the eyes of a falcon and the optimism of a Sancho Panza. We walked to St. Olaves and Fritton, Ellis revelling in wild flowers. Friend Cubitt lent us a boat, and we rowed and counted grebes, of which we saw young and old a score on an eighth of the lovely lake's area. Ellis bagged an uncanny water-insect - *Ranatra linearis* very like a daddy longlegs of the land. Ringdoves flip-flapped away at our intrusion. On the White House lawn that slopes from Mr. Cubitt's home to the lake a party of flycatchers acrobatted after white butterflies and flies, their youngsters sitting upon an iron rail and begged for them. A boatman asserted that fifty pairs of grebes were about, which seems unbelievable; and that a crossbill had been found drowned. Some cormorants roosted on the trees at night. Now, dinner at the Anglers' Tavern, and some lightning sketches for the landlord.

Then through Sandy Lane to Belton. Ellis, who used to be a carrier-boy to two Guernsey entomologists, rattled off the names of various butterflies which we saw in swarms; various whites, ringlets, gamekeepers, small heaths and coppers, holly blues - the second brood - small tortoiseshells, graylings, that have a habit of luffing, when settling on the earth. Here my henchman nabbed a lizard boxing him tail and all in an Oxo cube box. Natterjack toads trotted across the sandy land, here and there one peering out of its burrow.

A natterjack won't eat cinnabar caterpillars; the fine hairs tickle its throat. And hungry natterjacks occasionally gobble up an infant one, and finding out their mistake, actually spit them out again. Grey linnets of rosy-breast chortled on the hawthorn sprigs; a carrion crow squawked caution of us, and sparrows in their hundreds - summer lodgers in the cornfields, were in every corn patch.

On gay yellow ragworts striped Cinnabar caterpillars feasted; and as we gathered some - prickly hairs notwithstanding - a great dragonfly chased a butterfly but it eluded him. A large horseshoe bat flitted above the covert at 2.15 p.m. in bright sunshine. The flies! They followed us like swarming bees. I tried a noted ointment on my face: alas! it had the opposite effect; and until I had stuck a few small bracken leaves around my hat I had no peace.

Natterjack Toad

We crossed the common through the glorious bracken and heather; we hunted for adders; Ellis found one, but it escaped in the tangled undergrowth. A few days ago he fell in with four. "Cotton-tails" bolted as rabbits fled. On reaching my "little bit of fen," Tom (Brookes) was found admiring his young celery. On some prickly thistles hosts of five-spotted burnet moths fluttered and slept. Tom saw several crossbills yesterday, and several herons roosted in the trees across the ditch. Last night wading migrants broke the darkness with their shrill calls, whimbrel and godwits chiefly piping. At five o'clock we gave up our tickets at Southtown Station. The meanest countryside is like:

"All Eden bright.
With these her holy offspring,
Creations of the light;
As though some gentle angel,
Commissioned love to bear
Had wandered o'er the green sward
And left her footprints there."

Too much of a good thing!   Heron with eel

Chapter 25
JOHN KNOWLITTLE, NATURALIST

"I saw plainly, I should not know too much in the great field: I could hope to know but little, hence my coupling of the two words."

Arthur Patterson

Arthur H Smith wrote a "sketch" of Arthur in *The Naturalists' Journal*, in December 1901. This is his description:

It is easy to picture a wiry, slightly-bowed man, with the profile of an artist of romance, standing where reeds and rushes bow over still waters, intently watching the movements of a rare visitor to Broadland; or to imagine him plodding through a marsh swamp, his hat tilted to the rear and a useful stick tucked under his arm, while he holds a pair of field glasses ready for service. If he has a companion there will be an occasional remark in staccato, a linnet-like movement of the head, or an exchange of opinion regarding the identity of something seen in the distance.

Perhaps the swamp gives place to a path by the river, and after a short resting walk on comparatively firm ground he will cautiously peer over the crest of the river wall, resuming his walk with an Indian growl of discontent, or a brief description of the birds on the mud flats. Perhaps a sturdy marsh farmer, making a detour of his territory, will join him and speak in eloquent broad Norfolk dialect of "a Spune-bill" or the plumage of a hawk.

But any attempt at unimportant small talk is invariably confounded with a curt "Good morning," and Arthur resumes his walk in the manner of one who must cover within an hour or so a given number of miles.

Arthur's face was full of character, with distinctive high brow, aquiline features and beard of an artist. His skin, sculptured by the elements, was wrinkled and weather-beaten. His eyes were brown, bright as a hawk, searching and kindly with a touch of fire and dignity in their glance, which drew disciples. He was a quaint, extraordinary personality, and I was told, a cheery companion with a dry, almost sarcastic sense of humour. He was completely unassuming in nature and remained humble all his life in spite of his talents. He was a man who always enjoyed himself, living life to the full and thanking God each day he passed the aged of three score years and ten.

His "den", the front room of his last home, Ibis House, Lichfield Road, Yarmouth was out-of-bounds to all but his closest naturalist friends. The shelves bulged with his extensive library, filed systematically, wildlife pictures adorned the walls, and in corners were specimen jars, butterfly nets, fishing rods, and all his other paraphernalia. He always "booked up" before retiring, and often fell asleep with his pen in his hand. Family meals, if he joined them, were eaten in silence, otherwise he wrote at his desk. When money was short, he wrote on anything he could lay his hands upon, even wastepaper from his workplace was put to good use.

Arthur adopted the pseudonym "John Knowlittle" around 1896, under which he wrote in local papers. The reason was, he said:

A naturalist should be a specialist as a botanist, ornithologist, or entomologist. He may excel and in time be absolute master of his subject. I could see this, but my mind is not a concentrative one, and I want change, variety and a vaster enjoyment. I prefer to dabble in every nature puddle, as far as my own east coast corner is concerned. At his best a man can only grasp the fringes of any department of natural history in the course of a long laborious lifetime. Want of a scientific education, leisure, and not least - of means, were all against me. I have had my ups and downs, but I do not entertain one solitary grudge against fate.

Someone said of him: *"Always a lively and entertaining companion, with a sense of humour that served him well in his difficult early life and ensured him a hearty welcome wherever and whenever he was with friends. The life he loved was that he spent alone, or with a congenial companion in his houseboat – beside the waterfowl-frequented Breydon mudflats or in cruising in the "Yarwhelp" on rivers and broads. There he was at home, yet there was nothing of a recluse about him for he was always making friends."*

Arthur Patterson's grave in Gorleston Cemetery.
On the 50th anniversary of his death, a group met to remember him.
In the picture (back, left to right) the late John Makepeace, the late John Tooley,
David Ferrow, Sarah and Michael Bean.
(Kneeling, left to right) Peter Allard, Beryl Tooley, Ted Ellis and the late Arthur Lark.
(picture courtesy of Ivan Gould)

Arthur Henry Patterson finally put down his pen on October 27, 1935. Many tributes flooded in, amongst them were the following:

"We shall miss him and his work much, not only for what he did, but also for the energy he imparted to others."

"He left, as a legacy to the literature of Norfolk, books showing a mastery of his chosen fields, all distinguished by clear, incisive writing."

Arthur Patterson was laid to rest in Gorleston Cemetery, next to his beloved wife, Alice; a simple granite stone marks his grave. Amongst the tributes was placed a bunch of Breydon grasses, reeds and flowers picked by Ted Ellis that morning from the banks of Arthur's beloved Breydon.

Arthur once said:

The lives of good, interesting and unique individuals never ought to pass away unnoticed into oblivion. I do not suppose I have accomplished anything unusual or noteworthy, but I have derived immense pleasure from my pursuit of nature.

Had my opportunities and worldly circumstances been more enviable, I might have done better. As it is, I have done my best.

"FORTY WINKS!" AVOCETS

"Avocets on Breydon"

BIBLIOGRAPHY

References have been made to the publications listed in Part 1. This is not an exhaustive list of articles and pamphlets written by Arthur Patterson. His other published books are listed in part 2.

Part 1

1891   Royal Agricultural Hall, Islington. "First appearance in London of the great Rorqual whale captured at Great Yarmouth". pp. 8. Yarmouth: East Norfolk Printing Co., n.d. 1891

1896   "A protest by a masculine naturalist (Fur, fin and feather leaflets, No. 7: feminine head-gear: the Goura mount)". Illus., pp.4. Croydon: Society for the Protection of Birds, (1896).

1898-   "The Mercury Cartoons". A. Patterson's *Yarmouth Mercury*
1914   Cartoons relating to local politics and events.

1901   "The Caister Lifeboat Disaster". Cover picture for *"Supplement to Yarmouth Mercury."* November 18th, 1901. Great Yarmouth Printing Co. Ltd.

1901   "Catalogue of the Birds of Great Yarmouth, giving a few descriptive notes, and dates when most of the rarer species were obtained". 12 x illus. pp. (iv), 59, Yarmouth: Great Yarmouth Printing Co. 1901. (100 copies reprinted from the *"Zoologist"(*1900) for private circulation). The "catalogue" is preceded by an account of "The Birds of Great Yarmouth and neighbourhood" (pp. 1-20)

1901   "Yarmouth 100 years ago". In *"Yarmouth Independent,"* 1901.

1901   "Life of Charles H. Harrison, Broadland Artist: a memoir by A.H. Patterson and A.H. Smith". Ports., illus., pp. 60. (Edition limited to 175 copies). London: Jarrold and Sons (1903).

1903   "From Hayloft to Temple: The story of Primitive Methodism in Yarmouth, biographical, reminiscent, chronological, etc". Ports., illus., pp. xvi, 175. London: Robert Bryant, (1903).

1902   "The School Attendance Gazette, June 1902

1904   "Notes of an East Coast Naturalist: A series of observations made at odd times during a period of twenty-five years in the neighbourhood of Great Yarmouth". Illus. in colour by Frank Southgate, R.B.A, pp. xiii, 304. London: Methuen and Co. (1904).

1905	"Nature in Eastern Norfolk". 12 x colour illus. By Frank Southgate, R.B.A. pp. 352. London: Methuen and Co. (1905).

1905   "Nature in Eastern Norfolk". 12 x colour illus. By Frank Southgate, R.B.A. pp. 352. London: Methuen and Co. (1905).

1907   "Wildlife on a Norfolk Estuary", with preface by Her Grace the Duchess of Bedford. Line illus. by author, pp. xv, 352. London: Methuen and Co. (1907).

1909   "Man and Nature on Tidal Waters". Ports., illus., pp. xvi, 315. London: Methuen and Co. (1909).

1907   "Book of the Open Air: British Country Life in Spring and Summer", edited by Edward Thomas. Illus. vol. 1, pp. 56-63, 175-183; vol. 2, pp. 41-49, 107-120. London: Hodder and Stoughton, (1907).

1910-   "Chats about the Birdies. Chapters for Young Naturalists". In
1914   Springtime," *Primitive Methodist Pub. Ltd.*

1912   "A souvenir commemorating "My Twenty Years' Work as an Attendance Officer". (Limited to 100 copies printed by *Arthur Patterson* for private circulation). (November 1912).

1920   *"The Carrow Works Magazine"*, (Jan. 1920).

1925?   "Brundall on the Broads, an ideal river trip". Presented with the compliments of *The Brundall Gardens Steamship Co. Ltd.* Illus. with advertisements of local companies. pp.14. Yarmouth: C.A. Campling Ltd., Hall Plain, Great Yarmouth.

1921   "Holiday Nights and Days on Breydon". In *"Norwich Mercury"* series," (July – Sept. 1921).

1927   "Recollections of life in the Sixties and Seventies". In *"Yarmouth Mercury"* and *"Eastern Daily Press"*, (1927).

1929   "Wild-fowlers and Poachers: fifty years on the East Coast". Illus. 25 by author, 12 other, end-paper map. pp. xiv, 284. London: Methuen and Co. Ltd. (1929).

1930   "A Norfolk Naturalist: observations on birds, mammals and fishes". Illus. 35 by author and a frontispiece from painting of Charles H. Harrison. pp. xii, 209. London: Methuen and Co. Ltd. (1930).

1933   "Some old Yarmouth Sportsmen". In *"Yarmouth Mercury,"* 29 articles. (1933).

1934   "Bits of old-time Yarmouth. Series of articles recalling Arthur Patterson's childhood and youth". In *"Yarmouth Mercury,"* (1934)

1985   "John Knowlittle, the Life of the Yarmouth Naturalist, Arthur Henry Patterson, A.L.S.", by Beryl Tooley. Port., illus. pp.ix, 147. Norwich: Wilson-Poole Publishers (1985).

Part 2

1884   "Descriptive catalogue of the zoological department of the Preston Pleasure Gardens. Written and compiled for the convenience of visitors (by A.H. Patterson.)". Illus., pp. 31. Preston: H Oakey, (1884).

1887   "Seaside Scribblings for visitors; or, how to make the most of a holiday jaunt". Illus., pp. 139. London: Jarrold and Sons, n.d. (1887).

1888   "Notes on pet monkeys and how to manage them". Illus. by F. Lydon, pp. 105. London: L. Upcott Gill, n.d. (1888).

1889   Popular Sketches for the sea-beach and fireside. pp. 159. Gt. Yarmouth: A.N. Huke and Co.; London: Simpkin, Marshall and Co., n.d. (1889)

1889   "The Amateur's Zoo; or, pet animals, their habits, characteristics, and how to keep and treat them in captivity (Dean's practical guide book)". Illus., pp. 110 (ii). London: Dean and Son, n.d. (1889).

1891   "Fish-hook and float: salt water fishing and fresh water angling round about Yarmouth, a book for the visitor angler". Illus., pp. 62. Great Yarmouth: Stuart C. Blake. (1891).

1892   "Broadland Scribblings: a leisure-book for the holidays. By a Broadland naturalist." Illus., pp (viii), 198. Norwich: P. Soman and Son, (1892).

1892   "A list of the fishes of the Great Yarmouth district; with notes on each species". By "Luberta." Illus., pp. 62. Lowestoft: J. Rochford O'Driscoll, (1892).

1895   "Man and Nature on the Broads". Illus., pp.143. London: Thomas Mitchell, n.d. (1895).

1895   "Shadow Entertainments and how to work them; being something about shadows and the way to make them profitable and funny". Illus., pp. 76. London: Upcott and Gill, n.d. (1895)

1896   "Rambles in Birdland". Illus., pp.127. London: Thomas Mitchell, n.d. (1896).

1910   "Rough notes on the fish and fisheries of East Suffolk". Illus. by author, pp. (vi), 55. Great Yarmouth: John Buckle 1910 (111 copies reprinted from the *"Zoologist"* (1909) for private circulation with 14 illustrations and a map by the author.)

1920   "Through Broadland in a Breydon Punt" by John Knowlittle (A.H.P.). Illus. pp. xvi, 112, with preface by G. Christopher Davies. Norwich: H.J. Vince. (1920).

1923   "The Cruise of the 'Walrus' on the Broads: a Broadland Voyage in a North-sea Ketch-boat". Preface by Walter Rye. Illus., pp. 175. London: Jarrold Publishers (London) Ltd. (1923).

1930   "Through Broadland by Sail and Motor". Port., illus., pen and ink drawings by author, pp. vi. 141. London: *Blakes Ltd.,* (1930).

1930   "In Norfolk Bird Haunts in A.D. 1755". Reprinted from the *"Norfolk Chronicle"* Series. Illus. with pen and ink sketches by the author, pp. 103. Holt, Norfolk: Rounce and Wortley (1930).

GW00470246

WORLD PREMIERE
AN ABBEY THEATRE COMMISSION

TOWN IS DEAD

A PLAY WITHIN MUSIC

WRITTEN BY PHILLIP MCMAHON
MUSIC BY RAYMOND SCANNELL

Premiered on the Peacock stage on 8 June 2016

The Abbey Theatre gratefully acknowledges
the financial support of the Arts Council of
Ireland and the support of the Department
of the Arts, Heritage and the Gaeltacht.

ABBEY THEATRE AMHARCLANN NA MAINISTREACH

THE ABBEY THEATRE is Ireland's national theatre. It was founded by W.B. Yeats and Lady Augusta Gregory. Since it first opened its doors in 1904 the theatre has played a vital and often controversial role in the literary, social and cultural life of Ireland.

We place the writer and theatre-maker at the heart of all that we do, commissioning and producing exciting new work and creating discourse and debate on the political, cultural and social issues of the day. Our aim is to present great theatre in a national context so that the stories told on stage have a resonance with artists and audiences alike.

In 1905, the Abbey Theatre first toured internationally and continues to be an ambassador for Irish arts and culture worldwide.

Over the years, the Abbey Theatre has nurtured and premiered the work of major playwrights such as J.M. Synge and Sean O'Casey as well as contemporary classics from Sebastian Barry, Marina Carr, Bernard Farrell, Brian Friel, Thomas Kilroy, Frank McGuinness, Tom Mac Intyre, Tom Murphy, Mark O'Rowe and Billy Roche.

We support a new generation of Irish writers at the Abbey Theatre including Richard Dormer, Gary Duggan, Shaun Dunne, Stacey Gregg, Nancy Harris, David Ireland, Jimmy McAleavey, Owen McCafferty, Phillip McMahon, Elaine Murphy, Sean P. Summers, Michael West and Carmel Winters.

None of this can happen without our audiences and our supporters. Annie Horniman provided crucial financial support to the Abbey in its first years. Many others have followed her lead by investing in and supporting our work.

We also gratefully acknowledge the financial support of the Arts Council.

IS Í AMHARCLANN NA MAINISTREACH amharclann náisiúnta na hÉireann.

W.B. Yeats agus an Bantiarna Augusta Gregory a bhunaigh í. Riamh anall ón uair a osclaíodh a doirse i 1904, ghlac an amharclann ról an-tábhachtach agus, go minic, ról a bhí sách conspóideach, i saol liteartha, sóisialta agus cultúrtha na hÉireann.

Tá an scríobhneoir agus and t-amharclannóir i gcroílár a dhéanaimid anseo san amharclann, trí shaothar nua spreagúil a choimisiúnú agus a léiriú agus trí dhioscúrsa agus díospóireacht a chruthú i dtaobh cheisteanna polaitiúla, cultúrtha agus sóisialta na linne. Is í an aidhm atá againn amharclannaíochta den scoth a láithriú i gcomhthéacs náisiúnta ionas go mbeidh dáimh ag lucht ealaíne agus lucht féachana araon leis na scéalta a bhíonn á n-aithris ar an stáitse.

I 1905 is ea a chuaigh complacht Amharclann na Mainistreach ar camchuairt idirnáisiúnta den chéad uair agus leanann sí i gcónaí de bheith ina hambasadóir ar fud an domhain d'ealaíona agus cultúr na hÉireann.

In imeacht na mblianta, rinne Amharclann na Mainistreach saothar mórdhrámadóirí ar nós J.M. Synge agus Sean O'Casey a chothú agus a chéadléiriú, mar a rinne sí freisin i gcás clasaicí comhaimseartha ó dhrámadóirí amhail Sebastian Barry, Marina Carr, Bernard Farrell, Brian Friel, Thomas Kilroy, Frank McGuinness, Tom Mac Intyre, Tom Murphy, Mark O'Rowe agus Billy Roche.

Tugaimid tacaíocht chomh maith don ghlúin nua Scríbhneoirí Éireannacha in Amharclann na Mainistreach, lena n-áirítear Richard Dormer, Gary Duggan, Shaun Dunne, Stacey Gregg, Nancy Harris, David Ireland, Jimmy McAleavey, Owen McCafferty, Phillip McMahon, Elaine Murphy, Sean P. Summers, Michael West agus Carmel Winters.

Ní féidir aon ní den chineál sin a thabhairt i gcrích gan ár lucht féachana agus ár lucht tacaíochta. Sholáthair Annie Horniman tacaíocht airgid ríthábhachtach don Mhainistir siar i mblianta tosaigh na hamharclainne. Lean iliomad daoine eile an dea-shampla ceannródaíochta sin uaithi ó shin trí infheistíocht a dhéanamh inár gcuid oibre agus tacaíocht a thabhairt dúinn.

Táimid fíor bhúich don tacaíocht airgeadais atá le fail ón Chomhairle Ealaíon.

There will be no interval.

PRODUCTION CREDITS

Writer and Director	Phillip McMahon
Music By	Raymond Scannell
Musical Director	Cathal Synnott
Set Designer	Paul O'Mahony
Lighting Designer	Sarah Jane Shiels
Costume Designer	Saileóg O'Halloran
Sound Designer	Ben Delaney
Movement Director	Megan Kennedy
Voice Director	Andrea Ainsworth
Casting Director	Kelly Phelan
Literary Manager	Jessica Traynor
Production Manager	Cliff Barragry
Stage Manager	Bronagh Doherty
Deputy Stage Manager	Jean Hally
Hair and Make-Up	Val Sherlock
Graphic Design	Mandy Horton
Poster Photography	Aidan Kelly
Rehearsal and Production Photography	Ros Kavanagh
Voice Artist	Ger Kelly
Sign Language Interpreter	Amanda Coogan

SPECIAL THANKS TO

Katie Honan, Ruth Westley, Rosaleen Linehan, Aideen Howard, John Fairleigh,
Adam Matthews, Aidan Kelly, Angela McMahon, Tom O'Dea, Seamus Wylie,
Wayne Jordan, Irish Theatre Institute, the Tyrone Guthrie Centre and Roma 2 on
Wexford Street. A very special thank you to Kate Stanley Brennan and Ger Kelly.

M•A•C Cosmetics for providing make-up
products for this production.

TOWN IS DEAD

A PLAY WITHIN MUSIC
WRITTEN BY PHILLIP MCMAHON
MUSIC BY RAYMOND SCANNELL

CAST (IN ALPHABETICAL ORDER)

Barbara Brennan	Ellen
Kate Gilmore	Katarina
Fia Houston-Hamilton	Rachel
Conall Keating	Will

MUSICIANS (IN ALPHABETICAL ORDER)

Danny Forde	Band Leader/Keyboards
Christiane O'Mahony	Harp
Conor Sheil	Clarinet/Bass Clarinet

Town is Dead was conceived and developed by Phillip McMahon and Raymond Scannell.

Please note that the text of the play which appears in this volume may be changed during the rehearsal process and appear in a slightly altered form in performance.

BIOGRAPHIES

Writer and Director
Phillip McMahon

Music By
Raymond Scannell

Cast
Barbara Brennan
Kate Gilmore
Fia Houston-Hamilton
Conall Keating

Musicians
Danny Forde
Christiane O'Mahony
Conor Sheil

Musical Director
Cathal Synnott

Set Designer
Paul O'Mahony

Lighting Designer
Sarah Jane Shiels

Costume Designer
Saileóg O'Halloran

Sound Designer
Ben Delaney

Movement Director
Megan Kennedy

PHILLIP MCMAHON
WRITER/DIRECTOR

THIS IS PHILLIP'S directing debut at the Abbey Theatre. He was Writer in Association at the Abbey Theatre 2009/10. His previous playwriting credits at the Abbey Theatre include *Alice in Funderland* and *Investment Potential*. Acting work at the Abbey Theatre include *The Rivals*, *Translations* and *The Mapmaker's Sorrow*. Other directing work includes *Dublin Oldschool* (Project Arts Centre), *I'm Your Man* (THISISPOPBABY/Project Arts Centre), *High Heels In Low Places*, *A Woman In Progress*, *All Dolled Up, In These Shoes?* (Panti/THISISPOPBABY), *The Year of Magical Wanking* (THISISPOPBABY) and *Rubberbandits Live Arena Show* (Electric Picnic 2011). Playwriting credits include *Elevator* (THISISPOPBABY), *Pineapple* (Calipo), *All Over Town* (THISISPOPBABY/Calipo) and *Danny & Chantelle (still here)* (THISISPOPBABY). Screen credits include co-producer/writer on *The Queen of Ireland* (Blinder Films). Phillip is one half of pop culture outfit THISISPOPBABY, wherein he was co-creator and co-curator of the *THISISPOPBABY* performance venue (Electric Picnic Music and Arts Festival), *Queer Notions* cross arts festival (Project Arts Centre) and *WERK* Performance/Art/Club (Abbey Theatre, IMMA, Melbourne Festival). As a teenager Phillip was a member of Dublin Youth Theatre, National Youth Theatre and Australian Theatre for Young People. Phillip was a producer of annual charity gala *24 Hour Plays Dublin* (Abbey Theatre), which raises money for Dublin Youth Theatre, and of the *Alternative Miss Ireland* pageant (Olympia Theatre), which raised money for HIV/AIDS charities across Ireland. Phillip McMahon is a participant in Irish Theatre Institute's *Six in the Attic* resource sharing initiative.

RAYMOND SCANNELL

MUSIC BY

RAYMOND PREVIOUSLY WORKED at the Abbey Theatre on *Alice in Funderland.* Other recent music engagements include *Walking Pale (*Junk Ensemble/Dublin Dance Festival/GPO Witness History) and *Far Away From Me* (The Ark). As writer/performer Raymond's work includes *Deep,* winner of Best Male Performer and Spirit of the Fringe nomination at the Dublin Fringe Festival 2013 (Maura O'Keeffe/Irene O'Meara) which toured to the Galway International Arts Festival, Kilkenny Arts Festival, The Dock, Riverbank Arts Centre, The Half Moon, Cáirde Arts Festival and Make a Move Festival (Jen Coppinger) and *Mimic,* winner of Best Male Performer at the Dublin Fringe Festival 2008 (Raymond Scannell/Tom Creed/ Cork Midsummer Festival) which toured to the Galway International Arts Festival, Kilkenny Arts Festival, Cork Midsummer Festival, Electric Picnic Music and Arts Festival, The Liss Ard, Fit-Up Festivals, and The Irish Arts Center New York, PS 122, New York COIL Festival, the Centre Cultural Irlandais Paris and the Bristol Old Vic Proms. Playwrighting includes *Losing Steam* and *Mix it Up* (Corcadorca Theatre Company), *Beats 'n' Pieces* (Commissioned by Rough Magic Theatre Company, SEEDS Initiative, produced by Meridian Theatre Company), *Two for Joy* (NAYD 'New-Stage Project') and *A Day in the Life of a Pencil* (Graffiti Theatre Company). Acting work includes *Famished Castle, Digging for Fire* (Rough Magic Theatre Company), *Infinite Lives* (Tobacco Factory Theatres, Bristol), *Assassins* (Rough Magic SEEDS Showcase), *The Walworth Farce* (Druid Theatre world tour), *DRUID 35 Year Celebrations* (Druid Theatre 'From Galway to Broadway') and *The Silver Tassie* (Druid Theatre) at the Lincoln Center Festival, New York.

BARBARA BRENNAN
ELLEN

BARBARA'S PREVIOUS WORK at the Abbey Theatre includes *The Hanging Gardens*, *Shush*, *Big Love*, *Woman and Scarecrow*, *Lovers at Versailles*, *Down the Line*, *A Life*, *The Colleen Bawn*, *Kevin's Bed*, *A Picture of Paradise*, *The Importance of Being Earnest*, *A Woman of No Importance*, *She Stoops to Folly*, *Six Characters in Search of an Author*, *The Hostage*, *Angels in America*, *The Lilly Lally Show*, *Chamber Music*, *The Iceman Cometh*, *Drama at Inish*, *One Last White Horse* and *The Glass Menagerie*. Other theatre work includes *The Heiress*, Winner Irish Theatre Award for Best Actress 1979, *A Streetcar Named Desire*, Winner Irish Theatre Award for Best Supporting Actress 1981, *Hedda Gabler*, Irish Theatre Award nomination for Best Actress 1984, *Heartbreak House*, *Salomé*, *A Christmas Carol*, *Pygmalion*, *The Eccentricities of a Nightingale*, *Pride and Prejudice*, *The Beckett Festival*, *Festen*, *The Deep Blue Sea*, *Jane Eyre*, *Hayfever*, *Present Laughter*, *All My Sons* and *A Month in the Country* (Gate Theatre), *Cabaret* (Olympia Theatre), *By the Bog of Cats* (Wyndams Theatre, London), *Honour* (b*spoke theatre company), *Sleeping Beauty* and *Alice in Wonderland* (Landmark Productions), *Macbeth* and *The Making of 'Tis Pity She's a Whore* (Siren Productions), *Steel Magnolias* (Gaiety Theatre and National tour) and *Signatories* (Verdant Productions). Film and television work includes *The Clinic*, *No Tears* and *Hell for Leather* (RTÉ), *Veronica Guerin* (Merrion Film Productions) and *The Tudors* (Showtime Productions).

KATE GILMORE
KATARINA

THIS IS KATE'S debut at the Abbey Theatre. Other theatre work includes *The Train* (Rough Magic Theatre Company) at Dublin Theatre Festival 2015, *Breathless*, winner of the Irish Times Theatre Award in 2015 for Best Supporting Actress (ORion Productions and Danu Theatre Company), *Petals*, nominated for Best New Play at the Irish Times Theatre Awards 2015 (Roadkill Productions and Theatre Upstairs) and *Little Gem*, national tour (Breda Cashe Productions). Film and television work includes *The Legend of Longwood* (Grand Pictures), *Anna* (Viko Nikci) and *Fair City* (RTÉ).

FIA HUSTON-HAMILTON
RACHEL

THIS IS FIA'S debut at the Abbey Theatre. Other theatre work includes *Ghost the Musical* (GWB Productions/Base Entertainment Asia) and *Bare: The Rock Opera* (Paul Taylor Mills Ltd/Union Theatre London). Fia trained at Mountview Academy of Theatre Arts, London, where she performed in *The Heights* and *Into the Woods*. Other theatre work while in training includes *Cabaret* and *A Midsummer Night's Dream*.

CONALL KEATING
WILL

THIS IS CONALL'S debut at the Abbey Theatre. Other theatre work includes *A Boy Called Ned, Scars* and *Leper + Chip*, nominated and shortlisted for two awards at the Edinburgh Fringe Festival 2015 (Bitter Like A Lemon), *A Midsummer Night's Dream* (Fortunes Fool Productions) and *Dreamland* (Red Kettle). Conall graduated from the Gaiety School of Acting where he performed in *A Midsummer Night's Dream, The Playboy of the Western World, Punk Rock* and *Town and Country*. Film and television work includes *Love is Only Greed* (Coming Home Productions), *Meet Me* (AK Maganos), *The Jabberwocky* and *Embers* (Burn Sector Media), *Swept Away* and *Choices* (Headline Films), *The Sticks* (Ridley Scott Association Films/Black Dog Films) and *Fair City* (RTÉ). Conall was awarded a Special Commendation for Excellence in Acting and Performance by The National Youth Drama Festival in 2015. He will perform in *Measure for Measure* (Fortunes Fool Productions) in Dublin Castle and on an Irish tour in 2016.

DANNY FORDE
BAND LEADER/KEYBOARDS

THIS IS DANNY'S debut at the Abbey Theatre. Other theatre work includes *The Train, The Rise and Fall of the City of Mahagonny* and *How to Keep an Alien*, winner of Best Production at Dublin Fringe Festival 2014 (Rough Magic Theatre Company), *Unspoken* and *Assassins* (Rough Magic SEEDS), *Sleeping Beauty* (Lyric Theatre, Belfast), *The Last 5 Years* (Trees Rd.), *Sound Travels Under Water* (TEDx Fulbright), *MONSTER/CLOCK* and *The Aeneid* (Collapsing Horse), *Lusmór* (The Breakaway Project) and *Near Death: A Grim Reaper Musical* (Emerson College). Film work includes *Anna* (Safran Company), *Naken* (Dolores Film) and *Stitches* (Tailored Films). Danny is a songwriter and composer and currently performs with his bands Karmacloud and Everything The Light Touches.

CHRISTIANE O'MAHONY
HARP

CHRISTIANE PREVIOUSLY WORKED at the Abbey Theatre on *Pygmalion*. Other theatre work includes *The 24 Hour Plays* (Dublin Youth Theatre/The 24 Hour Company), *The Playboy of the Western World* (Druid Theatre), *Mary Stuart* (Pageant Wagon), *Ann and Barry* and *The Windstealers* (Dublin Fringe Festival) and *Orpheus* and *Sisters of the Rising* (Everyman Theatre). Television work includes *The Mario Rosenstock*

Show and *Holding out for a Hero* (RTÉ). She has a professional acting degree and a first class honours psychology degree from Trinity College, where she was a Foundation Scholar. She is also a first class honours graduate of the DipMus Programme at the Royal Irish Academy of Music. She has played all the major comedy clubs and festivals in Ireland and the UK as a stand up comedian. Her first play *Sisters of the Rising* is touring Ireland this year.

CONOR SHEIL
CLARINET/BASS CLARINET

THIS IS CONOR's debut at the Abbey Theatre. Other theatre work includes *Improbable Frequency* and *The Taming of the Shrew* (Rough Magic Theatre Company) and *Sweeny Todd* and *A Streetcar Named Desire* (Gate Theatre). Television work includes *The Irish Pub* and *Older Than Ireland* (Atom Films in association with Bord Scannan na h'Éireann). As an orchestral musician Conor has been engaged by the RTÉ National Symphony Orchestra, the RTÉ Concert Orchestra, the Irish Chamber Orchestra, and very many freelance groups. He has worked consistently in opera for Opera Theatre Company and for Wexford Opera Festival with whom he has enjoyed a long association.

CATHAL SYNNOTT
MUSICAL DIRECTOR

THIS IS CATHAL's debut at the Abbey Theatre. Other theatre work includes *Riverdance*, Broadway and international tours (Abhann Productions), *Blind Fiddler* (Lyric Theatre, Belfast), *Improbable Frequency* (Rough Magic Theatre Company), *Sweeney Todd* and *Threepenny Opera* (Gate Theatre), *Flatpack* (Ulysses Opera Company), *Into the Woods* and *The Cradle Will Rock* (The Lir Academy), *Once* (Landmark Productions) and *Christmas With the Priests*, Irish tour (The Priests). For five years Cathal was Singing and Musicianship/Choral Coach at the Lir Academy of Dramatic Art.

PAUL O'MAHONY
SET DESIGNER

PAUL's PREVIOUS WORK at the Abbey Theatre includes *Hedda Gabler, Major Barbara, The House, Pygmalion, Macbeth, The Seafarer, Fool for Love, Saved* and *Blue/Orange*. Other theatre work includes *Wuthering Heights, The Vortex, An Enemy of the People, Little Women* and *Faith Healer* (Gate Theatre), *Breaking Dad* and *Underneath the Lintel* (Landmark Productions), *The Talk of the Town* (Hatch Theatre Company, Landmark Productions and Dublin Theatre Festival), *Love and Money, Further Than the Furthest Thing, Pyrenees, Blood* and *The Country* (Hatch Theatre Company), *Dancing at Lughnasa* (Lyric Theatre, Belfast, and Dublin Theatre Festival), *A View From the Bridge*

(Everyman Playhouse, Liverpool), *The Importance of Being Earnest, Solemn Mass for a Full Moon in Summer, Is this About Sex?* and *Don Carlos* (Rough Magic Theatre Company), *The Girl Who Forgot to Sing Badly* (The Ark/Theatre Lovett), *Medea* (Siren Productions), *Pineapple* (Calipo), *Celebrity* (Peer to Peer Theatre Company), *Black Milk* (Prime Cut Productions), *Benefactors* (b*spoke Theatre Company), *This is Our Youth, Wedding Day at the Cro-Magnon's, Roberto Zucco, This is Not a Life, Pale Angel* and *Self-Accusation* (Bedrock Productions), *Hades, The Two Houses, The Green Fool* and *Epic* (Upstate Theatre Project), *Buddleia* and *The Clearing* (The Lir Academy), *Dodgems* (CoisCéim Dance Theatre and Dublin Theatre Festival), *Grease* (Cork Opera House) and *Rusalka* (Lyric Opera). Paul trained at Dún Laoghaire IADT, Dublin and the Motley Theatre Design Course, London.

SARAH JANE SHIELS
LIGHTING DESIGNER

SARAH JANE'S PREVIOUS work at the Abbey Theatre includes *The Shadow of a Gunman* (co-production with Lyric Theatre, Belfast) and *Shibari* (Dublin Theatre Festival 2012). Other theatre work includes *Educating Rita* (Lyric Theatre, Belfast), *The Cradle Will Rock* (The Lir Academy), *She Knit the Roof* (Earigail Arts Festival), *Lessness* (TheEmergencyRoom), *BEES!, Jockey, CARE, Farm, Follow* (WillFredd Theatre), *Everything Between Us, The Critic, The House Keeper, Plaza Suite* (Rough Magic Theatre Company), *PALS, The Boys of Foley Street, Laundry, World's End Lane, Basin* (ANU Productions), *Dublin Oldschool* (Project Arts Centre), *How to Keep an Alien* (Sonya Kelly/Rough Magic Theatre Company), *With Raised Arms/Here Me Sing Your Song* (Liv O'Donoghue), *Tundra* (Emma Martin), *Dusk Ahead* (Junk Ensemble) and *Have I No Mouth, The Blue Boy* and *Silver Stars* (Brokentalkers). Sarah Jane began lighting in Dublin Youth Theatre, completing a BA in Drama and Theatre Studies (Trinity College Dublin), and the Rough Magic SEEDS3 programme. She is co-artistic director of WillFredd Theatre.

SAILEÓG O'HALLORAN
COSTUME DESIGNER

SAILEÓG PREVIOUSLY WORKED at the Abbey Theatre on *Shibboleth*, Dublin Theatre Festival 2015. Other theatre work includes *Embodied* (Dublin Dance Festival), *Chekhov's First Play* (Dead Centre), *Thirteen*, Irish Times Judges Special Award (ANU Productions) and *Wake* (Chamber Made Opera). Film and television work includes *Pebbles* (Jonathan Shaw), *Epic Ireland* (Digital Post), *Lost in the Living* (Ballyrogan Films), *Children of the Revolution* (RTÉ), *TB* (Square One Productions), *Witness to History* (Coco Television) and *The Inquiry* (DCTV).

BEN DELANEY

SOUND DESIGNER

BEN'S PREVIOUS WORK at the Abbey
Theatre includes *Tina's Idea of Fun, The
Waste Ground Party, Maeve's House,
Twelfth Night, The Dead, Bookworms*
(2012 and 2010), *Juno and the Paycock,
The Passing, The East Pier, The Plough and
the Stars* (2012 and 2010), *Christ Deliver
Us!, The Last Days of a Reluctant Tyrant,*
for which Ben and Conor Linehan won an
Irish Times Theatre Award for Best Sound
Production 2010 and *Tales of Ballycumber.*
He is a sound engineer and composer of
electronic music and has been working as
a sound technician at the Abbey Theatre
since 2008. He graduated from Trinity
College Dublin in 2007 with a Masters in
Music and Media Technology, specialising
in surround sound mixing and digital art.

MEGAN KENNEDY

MOVEMENT DIRECTOR

MEGAN PREVIOUSLY WORKED at the
Abbey Theatre on *Romeo and Juliet.*
Megan trained at Alvin Ailey Dance
Center in New York City and received
a B.A. Honours from Queen Margaret
University in Edinburgh. She is Co-
Artistic Director of multi-award winning
Junk Ensemble. Choreography for live
performance includes *Marble & Bread*
(Dance Limerick), Tchaikovsky's *Queen
of Spades Opera* (Edinburgh Festival
Theatre), Bram Stoker Festival and eX
Choral Ensemble (IRL). Performance
and choreography for film includes
Óiche Nollaig na mBan (RTÉ/TG4),
The Wake (Invisible Thread Films),
Blind Runner (Junk Ensemble/Dance
Ireland Commission), *Wonder House*
(Dublin Film Festival) and *Her Mother's
Daughter*s, Winner Best Actress in
the Capalbio Festival Italy (Dance on
Camera NYC/RTÉ Dance on the Box).
Megan has performed internationally
with Retina Dance Company (UK), Tanz
Lange (Germany), Firefly Productions
(Belgium), Storytelling Unplugged
(Romania) and Blast Theory (UK).
Other credits as a performer include
The Blue Boy and *On This One Night*
(Brokentalkers), *Faun* and *As You Are*
(CoisCéim Dance Theatre), *Everlasting
Voices* (Mouth on Fire), *Pale Angel*
(Bedrock Productions) and productions
for the Pavilion Theatre and the Ark.
She was Dance Artist-in-Residence in
Limerick in 2014/15. Megan is a Fellow
of Salzburg Global Seminar and the chair
of Dance Travels.

Abbey Theatre
Staff & Supporters

SENIOR MANAGEMENT TEAM

Director / CEO
Fiach Mac Conghail

**Director of Finance
& Administration**
Declan Cantwell

**Director of Public Affairs &
Advancement**
Oonagh Desire

Technical Director
Aisling Mooney

ABBEY THEATRE BOARD OF DIRECTORS

Dr Bryan McMahon (*Chairman*)
Jane Brennan
Dónall Curtin
Loretta Dignam
Deirdre Kinahan
Niamh Lunny
James McNally
Sheelagh O'Neill
Mark Ryan
Paul Smith

An Roinn
Ealaíon, Oidhreachta agus Gaeltachta
Department of
Arts, Heritage and the Gaeltacht

The Abbey Theatre gratefully acknowledges the financial support of the Arts Council /An Chomhairle Ealaíon and the support of the Department of the Arts, Heritage and the Gaeltacht.

Archive partner of the Abbey Theatre.

2016 Abbey Theatre Supporters

IN PARTNERSHIP WITH

ÉIRE IRELAND | 19.....20 **16**

PRINCIPAL FUNDERS

 Culture Ireland Cultúr Éireann | 19.....20 **16** | Clár Comórtha Céad Bliain Centenary Programme

 An Roinn Ealaíon, Oidhreachta agus Gaeltachta **Department of Arts, Heritage and the Gaeltacht**

SUPPORTED BY

Roma Downey, Robert and Cynthia McCann, Thomas F and Carol O'Neill

TOWN IS DEAD

TOWN IS DEAD

WRITTEN BY PHILLIP MCMAHON
MUSIC BY RAYMOND SCANNELL

OBERON BOOKS
LONDON

WWW.OBERONBOOKS.COM

First published in 2016 by Oberon Books Ltd
521 Caledonian Road, London N7 9RH
Tel: +44 (0) 20 7607 3637 / Fax: +44 (0) 20 7607 3629
e-mail: info@oberonbooks.com
www.oberonbooks.com

A catalogue record for this book is available from the British Library.

PB ISBN: 9781783197989
E ISBN: 9781783197996

Design by Mandy Horton
Photography by Aidan Kelly

Printed and bound by 4edge Limited, Essex, UK.
eBook conversion by CPI Group (UK) Ltd, Croydon, CR0 4YY.

Visit www.oberonbooks.com to read more about all our books and to buy them. You will also find features, author interviews and news of any author events, and you can sign up for e-newsletters so that you're always first to hear about our new releases.

Town Is Dead is written to be performed within or without music. In its premier production, the play was presented 'within music', which is to say that much of the text, as written, was sung to Raymond Scannell's score. In this edition, blocks of text and various lines which appear italicised indicate repeats, refrains and harmonies which are sung. These should be omitted when the play is presented without music.

All action takes place in the living room of ELLEN's (68) flat. It's the middle flat of four flats in a three storey over basement tenement-style building on Dominick Street in present day inner-city Dublin. The room has basic furniture – a small couch, a standing lamp and a small TV tucked into the corner. There are doors which lead off to an unseen bedroom, and a hall door which leads out onto an unseen landing. There is one Georgian style window looming large on stage left. The room is filled with tattered boxes – crisp boxes, nappies boxes, and an array of German low cost supermarket boxes. ELLEN is moving, and her flat is all but packed up.

The play takes place over one afternoon into evening.

SCENE ONE

ELLEN's (68) living room-come-kitchen. Her son WILL (20) sits at the kitchen table. He wears a tracksuit more suited to the 1990s than today. He is a spirit, or a projection maybe, but that should not be apparent to the audience. He is seen only by ELLEN.

ELLEN enters, slamming the door.

ELLEN: Meddlin' bitch.

Can you believe that? I didn't know where to look.

Me own sister.

Standing there in her good frock, the vowels doing somersaults in her mouth.

You are welcome to stay with us in the interim – d'ye hear 'er?

Looking around at my furniture, like she'd gone and landed herself on the streets of Calcutta.

In the fuckin' what? Says I. What's an interim when it's at home?

WILL *laughs.*

Are you laughin' at me?

She *softens.*

I'll level with ya now, and I'm mortified saying it, but when she sez that, I got this knot of embarrassment or, I don't know – sadness maybe. I wasn't myself anyway.

WILL: *Hah hah hah hah.*

ELLEN: I felt all teary.

WILL: *Hah hah hah hah.*

ELLEN: And if you know one thing about me…is that…

I gave up the cryin' a long time ago.

I gave up the cryin' – didn't I?

I gave up the cryin' a long time ago.

This is me home though.

Change of tone – almost proud.

They're turning all this into offices, was I saying that? The inner city is not a kip any more.

We're living in prime real estate here. There where you're sittin', that'll be someone's desk. And me lamp there – that'll be one of them water coolers, with ice cold spring water on *tap*.

But, d'you know somethin'…

Our memories will be here, and no one will know.

WILL: *Our memories will live on*

BOTH: *In these walls.*

ELLEN: *Our memories will be stored,*
and no one will know.

WILL: *In these walls.*

BOTH: *Our memories will live on…*

ELLEN: 'Course it's not her, is it? She wouldn't know an 'interim' if it kicked her in the swiss. It's him – Francis. She's his parrot only. No, it's *him* all right. The kind of man who will die wonderin'.

ELLEN rummages in a packed box.

WILL: What are you doin'?

She pulls a dictionary out of a box.

ELLEN: *Gettin'* a proper indication of what that prick has in mind.

She lands on 'interim' in the dictionary.

It means – listen to this now – *interim* – a stopgap – between places, is what it means.

Well that's *that*, isn't it?

WILL: What's it?

ELLEN: He wants me put in a home.

> **WILL *laughs.***

You've no idea of him.

She can't piss, but he's under her feet, wantin' to know the whats, the whys and the wherefores. He's like a little weasel of a chess player – always planning his next few moves.

But he's a shock comin' to him, 'cos the nursin' homes'll only take you if your mind is goin' or you've enough poke to pay. It's all business at the end of the day.

Sharp as tack I am, and broke as a pauper, so fuck 'im.

I'll die in his box room if it's the last thing I do.

> **WILL *laughs at her gaffe.***

I'll die in that room – if it's the last thing I do. I'll die in that box room.

I'll die in that room – if it's the last thing I do. I'll die in that box room.

I'm still hoping you'll come with me.

I'm still hoping you'll come.

WILL: *I'll die in that room – if it's the last thing I do. I'll die in that box room.*

ELLEN: *I'm still hoping you'll come with me.*

I'm still hoping you'll come.

WILL: *You're gone in the head Ma – you're missing a screw. It's only a bedroom.*

> **KATARINA (23) bursts through the door. She is heavily pregnant, Croatian, but speaks with a broad Dublin accent. She is ELLEN's neighbour from upstairs.**

KATARINA: *(Panicked.)* Missus.

9

ELLEN: Would it kill you to knock on my jaysus door before allowin' yourself in?

KATARINA: Puko mi je vodenjak.

ELLEN: Do you wanna try that again in English?

KATARINA: Me waters just broke.

ELLEN: Fuck. What is it? Hot towels. Telephone. Where's Bobby?

> *ELLEN fishes down the sides of the couch. She's looking for her mobile phone. She's focussed on the task and not KATARINA, who is no longer panicked but stands behind ELLEN with a smirk on her face.*

That's all that curry sauce. After bringin' you on.

(To WILL.) Did you see my phone?

WILL/KATARINA: No.

> *ELLEN frantically opens boxes in search of the phone.*

ELLEN: I should have put labels on these. I'll never find anything.

> *Beat.*

I'm only after havin' me hand to it.

> *She pulls a tin of beans out of a box.*

Why am I packin' fuckin' beans?

> *KATARINA smirks. ELLEN stops in her tracks. She pauses before squinting in comical calculation.*

This a wind up?

KATARINA: It's a drill old lady. Checking you're not gone to mash potato up there.

ELLEN: Fuck ye. Out. I've enough to be doin' without lookin' at you.

> *WILL laughs.*

(To WILL.) You think that's funny, is it?

KATARINA: It's a laugh missus. You take life fierce serious.

ELLEN: You'd wanna catch yourself on. Get up. I've packin' to be doin'.

KATARINA: *(In a pleading tone.)* Ah don't be like that. I'm all Billy No Friends up there.

ELLEN: Where's Bobby?

KATARINA: Liftin'.

> *As in shoplifting. ELLEN shakes her head in disapproval.*

Shake your head all you like. Needs must.

ELLEN: *(Regarding KAT's bump)* Right *from wrong.* There's nothing else with kids. The rest is decoration. *Love* – all that – means fuck all in the end. Right from wrong – and that stops with you.

> *The half broken doorbell of the house buzzes.*

KATARINA: I don't know why I bother comin' down here…

ELLEN: Are you gettin' that door or wha'?

KATARINA: *(Leaving.)* …takin' the bleedin' head off me.

> *KATARINA exits.*

ELLEN: *(To herself.)* Winding *me* fuckin' up.

> *Beat.*

WILL: Number One Mum, is it?

ELLEN: Shut up you now. Isn't she gettin' the benefit of my experience?

WILL: Fountain of bleedin' knowledge.

> *KATARINA enters.*

KATARINA: You have a visitor.

ELLEN: For me?

KATARINA: Will I bring 'er up?

11

ELLEN: Me sister?

KATARINA: Don't think so.

ELLEN: Who's it?

> *KATARINA shrugs.*

Oh God. Official looking? Is her hair done?

KATARINA: She's not Irish.

ELLEN: What? Oh no. I don't know anyone like that. Tell her I'm not in.

RACHEL: *(Offstage.)* Hello?

> *RACHEL (29) enters. She's English, mixed-race, and speaks with a Birmingham accent.*

I followed. Sorry.

> *ELLEN and KATARINA stare at the stranger.*

(To ELLEN.) I don't mean to disturb you, but/

ELLEN: /Whatever it is you're looking for, I don't have it.

RACHEL: You're Ellen?

ELLEN: Gas, water, electric. Money? I don't have it.

> *ELLEN picks up the tin of beans.*

If you take magic beans, you're welcome to these.

> *She holds the beans at arms length.*

RACHEL: I started wrong I think.

KATARINA: I'll have them.

> *KATARINA snatches the beans. RACHEL is flushed.*

RACHEL: Can I take my coat off?

ELLEN: Do as you wish love, but you're not stoppin'.

RACHEL: Um.

> *Beat.*

Would it be okay if I sat down?

ELLEN: No.

RACHEL stumbles.

KATARINA: What in the hell?

ELLEN: What's all this about?

RACHEL begins to sob. The two women stare at her.

RACHEL: I'm sorry. I'm okay.

ELLEN: I don't care what you are, I just don't want it in my flat.

RACHEL composes herself.

RACHEL: My Dad died see/

ELLEN: /Oh/

RACHEL: /A fortnight ago, yeah. I keep bursting into tears when I least expect it.

ELLEN: Right, well…

RACHEL: I hadn't planned on starting like that.

ELLEN: Take off your coat. Whatever.

RACHEL takes her coat off. The women stand, unsure of what to do next.

I'll get you a cup of tea, will I?

RACHEL: I don't mean to be a nuisance.

ELLEN moves to find the kettle which is packed in a box.

ELLEN: Your work wouldn't be too happy with you crying in my front room I'd say?

RACHEL: My what?

ELLEN: *(Upending a packed box.)* I only had me hand to that fuckin' kettle.

(She spots it.) Ah.

She pulls out a kettle but the plug has been cut off.

What did I use that on?

WILL: For the heater.

ELLEN: For the heater, yeah.

RACHEL: I don't need the tea.

ELLEN upends another box. She pulls out a half bottle of whiskey.

ELLEN: You'll have a drink.

RACHEL: No.

ELLEN: We'll have a drink. Your Da in the ground an' all that. We won't rat you out to your/

KATARINA: /I'll have one.

ELLEN: You will in your eye.

(To RACHEL.) Sit.

ELLEN pours two whiskeys.

What was your name love?

RACHEL: Rachel.

ELLEN pushes a whiskey towards RACHEL. ELLEN raises a glass.

ELLEN: To your Father, Rachel.

RACHEL: Rachel Walsh.

ELLEN: May he rest in peace.

Beat.

RACHEL doesn't drink. Instead she watches ELLEN inhale the whiskey.

RACHEL: Do you know who I am?

Beat.

KATARINA: Is that to the whole room?

Pause.

RACHEL: Do you?

Beat.

ELLEN: *(Sternly.) Do* I?

RACHEL: You knew my Dad.

Pause. ELLEN stares at the young woman.

ELLEN: I don't think so.

RACHEL: My Dad is Sean.

Beat.

ELLEN: Who?

RACHEL: My Dad is Sean.

ELLEN: *(Shocked.)* Sean?

RACHEL begins to sob.

Are you sure?

KATARINA: Who the fuck is Sean?

SCENE TWO

The living room, a little later. RACHEL is composed. ELLEN watches RACHEL not drinking her whiskey.

RACHEL: I don't drink.

ELLEN: Me neither, but we'll make an exception seeing as it's a Wednesday.

ELLEN drinks.

To Sean, I suppose.

RACHEL: My Dad never talked to me about Ireland, until the last days of his life.

ELLEN: Why is that?

RACHEL: Went crazy if you asked him. I don't know. That was just Dad.

ELLEN: Right.

RACHEL: But after the heart attack –
when we thought he'd pull through/

VOICES: *Ooh ooh ooh.*

RACHEL: /He asked me to go to the house, and find something in his room.

He kept almost every shred of paper that ever touched his hand. The clean up in his house after he died was…it was disgusting. Take-away menus a decade old – that kind of thing – it was very upsetting.

WILL: *Ooh Ooh Ooh Ooh*
Ooh Ooh Ooh Ooh
Ooh Ooh Ooh Ooh

> *KATARINA enters. She's eating beans from a bowl.*

ELLEN: *(Sniffing.)* What's that?

KATARINA: Them beans.

ELLEN: Your gas on?

KATARINA: They're cold.

ELLEN: Smell o' them.

KATARINA: *(Proudly to RACHEL.)* I'm pregnant.

RACHEL: Yeah.

KATARINA: *And* I'm fuckin' starvin'. Bobby better have all manner of cream cakes and battered sausages when he walks up them stairs.

ELLEN: Dream on.

KATARINA: Is right.

> *Pause.*

RACHEL: But it was a photograph – the thing. It was in a biscuit tin in his wardrobe, and it was a picture of you and Dad at Dudley Castle.

ELLEN: Where?

> *RACHEL takes the photo from her bag. She hands it to ELLEN. KATARINA cranes for a look.*

KATARINA: Is that a corkscrew perm?

> *ELLEN is taken aback at the sight of the image.*

I'm scarlet.

RACHEL: When he showed it to me, I didn't understand. I flipped, 'cos I was confused. I was a real bitch to him. *Who are these people*, you know?

KATARINA: What's Dudley Castle when it's at home?

ELLEN: It's in Birmingham.

KATARINA: Posh.

RACHEL: Yeah. *Who are these people?* I was furious. And then he told me about you.

> **Beat.**

ELLEN: Is this some joke?

RACHEL: You don't believe me? The colour of my skin?

ELLEN: I don't know.

RACHEL: I've got pictures.

> *RACHEL reaches for her bag. ELLEN raises a hand to stop her.*

ELLEN: Sean/

RACHEL: /Dad.

> **Beat.**

ELLEN: It was a long time ago.

RACHEL: You *were* married to my Dad though.

17

ELLEN: *(Biting.)* In the eyes of the law sweetheart, I'm still married to him.

KATARINA: *(Mock startled.)* Oh.

ELLEN: *(Sarcastically.)* Did he leave me anything?

Pause. A stand off.

RACHEL: My husband doesn't know I'm here. I said I was going to Nuneaton with a friend. He thinks I'm being ridiculous. Looking for you.

ELLEN: Well.

RACHEL surveys the boxes scattered about the room.

I'm moving.

RACHEL: Oh. Why?

ELLEN: I bought a penthouse in Manhattan.

KATARINA: Gettin' hoofed out, the lot of us. Wanna change the locks if they want me out but.

ELLEN: Call the Guards is what they'll do.

KATARINA: Let them lock me up. Least I'll have a roof over me head.

ELLEN: *(To RACHEL.)* Look/

RACHEL: /Dad had a heart attack. I said that. We were at the seaside buying ice creams, and he just dropped down without warning.

ELLEN: Life gets you eventually.

RACHEL: In front of my girls. We have a caravan in Skegness. Nothing fancy, but my Brian likes to get out of Brum at the weekends. And Dad had started to come with us. I don't know why, 'cos he hated not sleeping in his own bed.

ELLEN: Hated fresh air, if memory serves.

RACHEL recognises this.

RACHEL: I thought he was dead. There on the sand. Lying like a sack of potatoes. His hand clamped at his neck. I thought, this is it, this is *the moment that every child dreams about.* Is that weird?

ELLEN: It's a complex thing with kids.

RACHEL: I look at my daughters and I think – you're gonna hate me one day.

ELLEN: Drink some of that whiskey there.

RACHEL doesn't drink.

RACHEL: I was a mistake I think.

ELLEN: *(Dismissing.)* Ach.

Beat.

RACHEL: Mum was *touched in the head* – If you were to believe my Dad. *Not all there,* and that'd be the end of it.

Left when I was in nappies, so not there at all.

Pause.

Do you mind me talking like this?

ELLEN: Like what?

RACHEL: He spoke about *you.*

ELLEN: Ah now.

RACHEL: He didn't die there on the sand, see. We rushed him to the hospital – and it looked, for a minute, like he was going to be okay. He was sitting up and –

He talked more in those few days –

And he told me about you. And about the boy in the picture.

The mention of the boy hangs in the air.

KATARINA: Who is it?

Beat.

ELLEN: My William.

KATARINA: Oh.

RACHEL: Yes.

> Dad told me about you and about William.
>
> Out of nowhere.
>
> I didn't take it well.
>
> I think that's why my husband, Brian, who thinks I'm in Nuneaton, I think that's why he thinks it's ridiculous me looking – 'cos I was a cow about it with Dad. I was heartbroken. Selfish I suppose, but I felt like I never knew him then, and he was all I had for a very long time. And I suppose I thought he'd robbed me of something with William – me being an only child and that.

ELLEN: *(Anxious.)* What about my William?

WILL: Go easy Ma.

RACHEL: But he said, Dad. He said, *you're going to want to meet them.*

WILL: *You're going to want to meet them.*

RACHEL: That's the kind of person I am see, once I calm down.

> And he said to say that he's sorry.

WILL: *And he said to say that he's sorry.*

> *You're all I've got.*
> *You're everything.*
> *You're all I've got.*
> *The start and the end.*

RACHEL/WILL: *You're all I've got.*
> *You're everything.*
> *You're all I've got.*
> *The start and the end.*

ELLEN: Why are you telling me this?

RACHEL: When he said William's name, he nearly choked. It was distressing to watch, 'cos he just wasn't like that.

Beat.

Because he's my brother.

ELLEN: **(Sharply.)** Your what?

RACHEL: William. I came to find him, didn't I?

Beat.

To see him, and to be seen I suppose.

ELLEN: You *have* your family.

RACHEL: What?

ELLEN: He's *not* your brother.

RACHEL: He is.

ELLEN: My William?

RACHEL: I'm not here to upset anyone. It's not like that.

ELLEN: But Will…

Beat.

RACHEL: **(Demanding.)** Please.

WILL: Don't milk it Missus.

ELLEN: Will is gone.

(Beat.)

He's dead a long time.

SCENE THREE

The living room. An hour later. ELLEN is alone with WILL. ELLEN is unpacking boxes in an effort to find something. The flat is beginning to resemble a jumble sale.

WILL: What are you up to? You have this kip upturned.

21

ELLEN: I can't find me pictures. Me album with all me photos in it. I want to show that girl. There's a lovely one of you making your confirmation, but I can't find the book.

WILL: Get a grip Ma. I'm wearing those bottle glasses in that picture.

ELLEN: I know. That's what I want to show her.

WILL: Don't make a laugh o' me. Show her one of the ones where, er, I'm looking smooth.

Beat.

Here Ma?

ELLEN: What?

WILL: Are you after gettin' the jump of your life?

ELLEN: You'd love that, wouldn't ya? I got a start, not a jump. So now. No. You have me ready for anything.

ELLEN gives up on the boxes.

I should have labelled these, but I didn't have the labels, and I didn't have the energy for going in to town.

WILL: Town is at the end of the road you mad thing.

ELLEN: But I can't face it any more.

ELLEN is agitated.

And you know what?

Once I close these boxes. Once I tape them up…

The boxes won't be opened ever again.

Francis'll have them in the attic.

My things. Locked away.

And I'll be dead then.

WILL: *Dead then.*

WILL laughs.

ELLEN: Laugh it up bucko, but that's all I have to look forward to.

> **Beat.**

I'm never seeing any of this/

WILL: /Shite.

ELLEN: *(Laughing.)* Shite. Exactly. I'm not seeing any of this shite again.

> *ELLEN sips on some whiskey.*

WILL: Having a drink, is it?

> *ELLEN stares into the glass.*

ELLEN: I'm having *one.*

> *RACHEL pushes through the door carrying two empty crisp boxes. KATARINA enters behind her sucking on an ice lolly and carrying an open packet of Monster Munch and an open packet of Manhattan Popcorn.*

(About the boxes.) That it?

RACHEL: Shopkeeper wasn't very forthcoming. Said to say that's your lot. Sorry.

ELLEN: *(To KATARINA.)* Where'd *you* get all that?

KATARINA: Your wan bought it for me.

ELLEN: You cheeky bitch.

RACHEL: I insisted.

ELLEN: He says what to you?

KATARINA: He says you better be planning on settling up with him before you hit that M50.

ELLEN: Excuse me?

KATARINA: Says you owe him a score for bottled gas.

ELLEN: I do in my bollox. I wouldn't waste me money in that hovel.

RACHEL: Should I have given it him?

ELLEN: What? No.

RACHEL: I could do it now.

ELLEN: Are you deaf? I don't owe the prick anything. Let him follow me to poxy Lucan.

RACHEL: Where?

ELLEN: Exactly.

KATARINA: Might as well be Mars.

ELLEN: Or Glasnevin.

Beat.

Twenty-seven years I'm here.

It's not right me goin'. Not like this.

RACHEL gathers courage.

RACHEL: What happened?

ELLEN: The landlord is a mean bastard.

KATARINA: And the rest.

RACHEL: With William –

ELLEN: I know. Give me a minute –

RACHEL: It's why I'm here –

Beat.

ELLEN: *(To KATARINA.)* Has Bobby whiskey up there?

KATARINA: How many times do I have to tell you; he's given it up.

Beaming at RACHEL.

We's gettin' our act together.

RACHEL: Right.

ELLEN: Her father just died.

KATARINA: Yeah. I'm not fuckin' deaf.

RACHEL: Oh/

ELLEN: *(To RACHEL.)* /She's Croatian. One of them
  immigrants.

KATARINA: Refugees.

ELLEN: Little nipper refugee, that's it, comin' over, weren't ya?

  And now she thinks the world owes her somethin'.

KATARINA: Owes me a fiver.

ELLEN: They're all like that I think.

KATARINA: *(Patting her bump.)* I'm Irish now, amn't I?

ELLEN: *Is* there booze up there?

KATARINA: Are you listening to me atall?

ELLEN: This girl/

RACHEL: /Rachel.

ELLEN: She's in bits. Look at her.

RACHEL: I'm fine./

ELLEN: /She's grievin', and she's gaspin' for a drink.

  (To RACHEL.) Aren't ye?

RACHEL: No.

ELLEN: She is.

> *ELLEN gives KATARINA a stern look. KATARINA
> makes to leave.*

KATARINA: It's on your head when Bobby comes in lookin'
  for it.

> *KATARINA exits. The women stand awkwardly
> about the room. ELLEN downs the last of her
> whiskey. She attempts to tidy some items back into
> their boxes.*

ELLEN: Not far from here we was reared – me and your Da/

RACHEL: I don't have much time is the thing.

ELLEN: Sit down.

/in houses not unlike this one.

Remembering.

Big old draughty rooms, with them fancy cornices on them. Is that what you'd call them? Cornices? Georgian anyway. The roof things.

And your Da's Da – your Granda I suppose – he was fierce proud of them cornices. He'd be havin' his dinner and he'd look up and say, 'Georgian they are', smilin' like he owndid the world. And Rosie, bless her, would have the words out of his mouth, so that she'd see a lovely pram in the street and she'd say, *That's only Georgian that is.*

Rosie – Rosie was your Granny – fierce good to me when me Mother passed, she was.

Ten then.

And another ten from then we was on a boat to England. 1968. Fresh married and looking for a start.

RACHEL: With Dad?

ELLEN nods. KATARINA enters with whiskey.

KATARINA: It looks like piss.

ELLEN: All goin' the same place. Give it here.

KATARINA hands ELLEN the whiskey. ELLEN pours it.

Half an education, and even less sense between us, me and Sean, getting on that boat. But we couldn't have stayed here. There was nothing doing.

KATARINA: What's this now?

RACHEL: *(Pressing a finger to her lip.)* Do you mind?

KATARINA: I live here. Who the fuck are you?

ELLEN: *(Snapping.)* You don't live here. Get that out of your head. I live here. You live upstairs – and not for much longer neither.

KATARINA: Don't get smart with me *you.* I'll lamp ye.

ELLEN: Sit down now and…chill out.

KATARINA sits.

KATARINA: *(To ELLEN.)* You'd wanna mind your graces.

Beat.

ELLEN: *(To RACHEL.)* We used to fight, me and him. Fallin' in and out of bars 'cross Birmingham, scrapping like dogs. Punching because holding didn't come natural.

Away from home and not a clue between us. Wayward we were.

And when the first baby was lost. Yeah. And the shock of that made us even wilder. Not far off animals we were.

And when the second one was lost – well, that put a stop to our carousing.

That put a stop to us all right.

That put a stop to us all together.

Boys they were, that came out of me – still. Boys that he wouldn't have me put names to…

Reading RACHEL's mood.

You're lookin' at me now.

I can tell you or I can not tell you. It's all the one to me.

RACHEL: Yeah. I need to know.

ELLEN: Sean went into himself then. He went very bad.

He was like a pig with the drinkin'. Sinkin' more pints than his body could hold, and his hands all loose on his return. And mine too at that. Like mongrels –

27

Heaping damage upon damage.

WILL: *Heaping damage upon damage*

ELLEN: But in the end he'd run out of steam, or money maybe. And he'd show up all quiet…

I'm sorry love.

The red mist fading around him.

We should go home.

WILL: *I'm sorry love.*
We should go home.
We were going nowhere.

ELLEN: There was no home to go to. Just England and Ireland. And none better than the other.

RACHEL: Dad wasn't violent.

ELLEN: What was he?

RACHEL: I don't know.

ELLEN: That your eulogy, was it?

RACHEL: Never raised a hand to me.

ELLEN: Let me tell you something. Your *Da* was a prick.

Beat.

And I was no better.

ELLEN pours whiskey.

Ah, we used to kill each other.

We'd fight and we'd fight.

But, we'd make up too.

But even that – being intimate – even that felt like fightin'.

Me body was aching for a baba, but. Me heart and me skin and me soul wanted it that much.

And I knew I could do it. I knew I had it in me.

WILL: *(Cheerleading.)* Go on Ma.

ELLEN: March 1st he popped out. 1974. Donnacha I called him/

KATARINA/WILL: Ew.

ELLEN: /And then I thought, no, I want him to be a little English boy. A good little English boy. So I called him William.

RACHEL: Will.

ELLEN: My Will, yeah.

     Beat.

Tell you one thing. A baby straightens ya.

(To KATARINA.) You mark my words.

RACHEL: Dad must have been made up.

ELLEN: He was working on the sites be then.

Yeah.

Worked every hour he could get, stackin' bricks.

KATARINA: That'll be my Bobby. I've warned him. *You're gettin' a fuckin' job whether you like it or not.*

ELLEN: Sean'd come home late. The child would be asleep. He'd have nothing to say. Then he'd be back out first thing. We never saw him.

RACHEL: Can't blame him for that. He had to work.

ELLEN: I was desperate lonely but. Depressed you'd call it now – but in them days you were just told get on with it.

No friends. No family. Neighbours wouldn't look at you. England was a different world. Just staring at a child, and puttin' up a dinner whenever he decided he'd had enough of the pub.

(Sarcastically.) It wasn't very fulfilling.

I'm gonna have to do something with meself, is what I was tellin' meself, or else I was done for.

RACHEL: So you walked out on him?

ELLEN: What? No. I got meself a little job, didn't I?

RACHEL: Did you?

ELLEN: And *he* went mad.

KATARINA: Your fella?

RACHEL: Why?

ELLEN: Spittin' he was. Wouldn't look at me.

> And the gettin' work wasn't easy. Not for a woman but certainly not for the Irish – not at that time.

> We were scum to the Brits.

> Ever since them bombs went off in them pubs, we couldn't hold our heads up in Birmingham.

> I loved me little job. Just a dirty kip of a pub in Snow Hill, cleaning toilets and pulling pints, but it was me own space. With me own friends.

> Like George.

GEORGE *appears in silhouette, upstage.*

> Ten years in Birmingham and a thought struck me one day while I was emptying ashtrays, so I says to Black George who I worked with – I says, *I never spoke with a black man before.*

GEORGE: *Next thing you know you'll be talking with queers.*

ELLEN: You're never?

GEORGE: Bent as a butcher's hook. Come out of the dark ages. It's 1978 love.

ELLEN: The Blacks and the Pakis and the Irish – We were all in it together at that time. But queers?

> George. Gorgeous George.

> Oh my God he was gorgeous, my gorgeous George.

He'd hold my freckled white skin 'gainst the dark of his arms.

You are a work of art, he says to me once.

And he was all of that to me too, my gorgeous George.

At home I said nothing. Went on as if work was just a task what needed doing. But every day was a new adventure.

We'd smoke fags, me and George, and I'd suck the life out of a boiled sweet on the way home to hide the smoke on me breath.

WILL/KATARINA: *La dee da da da da dah.*

La dee da da da da dah.

ELLEN: *Oh my God he was gorgeous, my gorgeous George.*

He'd hold my freckled white skin 'gainst the dark of his arms.

You are a work of art, he says to me once.

And he was all of that to me too, my gorgeous George.

Oh my God he was gorgeous, my gorgeous George.

He'd hold my freckled white skin 'gainst the dark of his arms.

You are a work of art, he says to me once.

And he was all of that to me too, my gorgeous George.

I lay down with him one time.

KATARINA: You fucked him? The black fella?

ELLEN: *(Snapping.)* That mouth of yours will be the undoing of you young one.

(ELLEN grins.) But, yeah – I did. And it was/

ELLEN *make a sound of an explosion.*

KATARINA: Urgh.

ELLEN: Nothing before or after ever matched it.

RACHEL: Did you really cheat on my Dad?

ELLEN: Don't go there with me girlo.

> It was a one time thing. A project to see if George could – with a *woman* like. And it turns out he could, and he was glad that he did, thank you very much.
>
> And we celebrated our silly experiment with bottled cider and cigarettes in the stock room. And it was the most *free* I ever felt in me life.
>
> So *don't* go there with me.
>
> George.
>
> I haven't said that name in years.
>
> He gave me courage.
>
> Yeah.
>
> He gave me strength.

KATARINA: You wild bitch.

RACHEL: Wild? It's horrible.

KATARINA: Is she for real?

ELLEN: *(To RACHEL.)* Say what you're sayin'.

Beat.

RACHEL: He didn't deserve that – to be treated like that. Dad was the way he was because of – you left him there.

ELLEN: There's a lot I've to live with when I look in the mirror.

RACHEL: My Dad was a good man.

ELLEN: None of us were good. Know that. Getting through it is all we were doing.

RACHEL: *(Upset.)* He *was* good.

Beat. A stand-off.

ELLEN: Who wants a sup?

KATARINA: You're gonna let her away with talkin' to you like that? If I as much as breathe, you're down me neck.

ELLEN: Whist now. This girl is/

RACHEL: /Family?

ELLEN: *(Laughing.)* Jaysus. Stop, will yiz.

(To RACHEL.) Are you havin' a sup?

KATARINA: I am.

ELLEN pours whiskey.

RACHEL: Is that okay?

ELLEN: No. And she knows it 'cos I'm forever telling her.

KATARINA: It's a sip.

ELLEN pours KATARINA some whiskey regardless.

RACHEL: *(Softening.)* Do you know what you're having?

KATARINA: Yeah. A baby.

ELLEN: This is the kind of nonsense I've to put up with.

KATARINA: You love it Ma.

ELLEN: You can quit all that tosh. I'm not your mother.

KATARINA: Grandma then.

ELLEN stops. Beat.

ELLEN: I'll not promise you nothin' now or nothin' right. But if you find your way out to Lucan…I'll consider it.

KATARINA sips on some whiskey, smiling.

But you won't be gettin' *that* out of me if that's what you're after.

RACHEL: What about your own mum?

KATARINA: *(Biting.)* Excuse me?

ELLEN: Don't set her off, please.

KATARINA: Says you. You haven't come up for bleedin' air.

Beat.

The mad bitch turfed me out on the street, when I was only sixteen.

(To ELLEN.) I know you old lady, you want to dress things up.

ELLEN: We're only hearing one side of that story. Mark my words.

KATARINA: Tell me the side of the story I'm missing?/

ELLEN: /I'm not sayin' that/

KATARINA: /What kind of nut job would you have to be to choose a made up man in the sky over your own flesh and blood?

'Cos as I passed that gate, with the rain pouring down on me/

WILL: *Down on me*
Down on me
Down on me

KATARINA: /and a ripped SPAR bag stuffed up with clothes, she screams after me:

Katarina. Ovo je Bozja volja.

ELLEN: She goes into that gobbledegook from time to time.

Beat.

KATARINA: *This is God's will.*

RACHEL: She never?

ELLEN: Welcome to Ireland. You'll have to visit the Guinness Factory.

RACHEL: What had you done?

KATARINA scoffs.

KATARINA: I made the baby Jesus cry.

(Beat.) I'd been having an affair/

ELLEN: /Joan Collins has affairs. You don't have affairs. You were having a greasy ride with your uncle down a lane.

KATARINA: Fuck off, it was in a house, and he's not me uncle.

ELLEN: What is he then?

KATARINA: We just *called* him uncle, but he's not *actually* me uncle. I don't know what he is.

ELLEN: A paedo.

KATARINA: Well. Yeah. But it's me who disgraced meself in the eyes of God.

ELLEN: 'Cos it was you was in trouble.

KATARINA: *(To RACHEL.)* I got pregnant off it.

RACHEL: So?

ELLEN: They weren't very understanding.

KATARINA: One way of putting it.

RACHEL: And you just, what, slept on the streets?

ELLEN: You met the love of your life on them streets.

(To RACHEL.) You want to talk about good men? Bobby's one of them.

KATARINA: You wouldn't want to see what I've seen. Life on the streets is fuckin' mingin'.

Four Courts, Smithfield, Capel Street – bedding down with all sorts.

Like this yoke of a thing tried to get me on side once, with promise of a place to stay full of *good girls just like me* – givin' it the full big sister. Wantin' me selling me body, turns out. To line *her* pockets.

RACHEL: Oh God.

KATARINA: Fuckin' relentless she was. Like a dog with a bone. I'd had enough of 'er harrasing but. Caught her by the throat one night – shocked at me own strength. Grippin' her wind pipe. The teeth janglin' in her head, the eyes bulgin' out of her skull. It was too easy – the drugs had her ravaged. I felt this power in me hands though. It was amazin', and I thought, I could end you. I'd be doing the world a favour.

Beat.

Turns out I'm too nice for that.

Left her cryin' an' gurglin' – thinking, *that'll be a lesson for 'er now.*

But some cunts never learn.

'Cos her bloke – her *man* – he caught up with me, didn't he?

Took me out for a batin'.

Throwing punches like Tyson. Up and down Church Street. People just watchin' on. Barristers, solicitors – that part of town. No one doin' nothin'. All just going about their business as as a fuckin' ape kicked the unborn baby out of a teenage girl.

Silence.

Me Ma came up to the hospital. With pyjamas and money. And I thought, she's come to take me home. It's just me now, so it's okay.

I says to her, I says *Mammy* – she loved it when I talked English to her – I says, *Mammy, will you forgive me? Will God forgive me?*

And she said…

I hope you understand the risk I've taken. If your father even knew I was here, I'd have hell to pay.

And then she was gone.

I know all about hell, me. I know all about hell.

If she'd seen the things that I've seen. I know all about hell.

I saw her years later down on Henry Street. I was lifting in one of the big shops – Arnott's I think. Make-up, or sprays or something, and I was looking around, scoping security, and me eye happened upon this woman shopping, and she was staring back at me. Now I must have looked in a million bits. I was roughin' it at the time, and I wasn't washing or anything. Me hair would have been like something out of a nature programme. But she smiled at me. A sad, pathetic, teary kind of a smile. But it was her, Majka.

I know all about hell, me.

WILL: *I know all about hell.*

KATARINA: *I know all about hell.*
If she'd seen the things that I've seen.

WILL: *I know all about hell.*

KATARINA: *I know all about hell.*
Believe me
Believe me

BOTH: *Believe me*
Believe me

KATARINA: *Believe me*
Believe me
Believe me

WILL: *I know all about hell, me. I know all about hell.*

You wouldn't believe the things that I've seen.

BOTH: *Believe me*

Beat.

RACHEL: What did you do?

KATARINA: Ran to the street.

Beat.

We was just strangers by then.

SCENE FOUR

The living room, a little later. KATARINA watches a battered old TV. She has earphones plugged into it, which means she has to sit very close to the screen, the light illuminating her face. ELLEN and RACHEL sit at the kitchen table.

RACHEL: I *am* in Nuneaton.

ELLEN: What is it love?

RACHEL: I said before. My husband thinks I'm in Nuneaton.

ELLEN: Yes. You said that.

RACHEL: It's 'cos I *am*. I'm staying with a friend.

ELLEN: Oh?

RACHEL: I don't know if I can go back.

ELLEN: What about your kids?

RACHEL: With their Dad. I can't help thinking I'm bad for them.

ELLEN recognises the impulse.

Did you leave my Dad?

ELLEN: Yeah.

RACHEL: Was it that bad?

ELLEN is quiet.

I didn't know him is the thing. I never asked him anything. About his life – nothing. That's me really.

Pause.

ELLEN: I had to.

RACHEL: Why though?

KATARINA butts in from beside the TV.

KATARINA: Don't set her off.

ELLEN: I'll be dug out of you.

KATARINA: It'll be the last thing you do.

38

Beat.

ELLEN: I was made manager of the Queen's Head. The pub.
This is years later. 1985.

KATARINA joins the conversation.

Stock take. Cash up. In my little boozer. You name it – I
was responsible for it.

My Sean was ragin' – went on like a child he did. He'd all
but stopped talking to me by that time.

Save for to get him his drink or put his dinner up.

And George – George was working in the bank by then.
He'd call in to the Queen's *every* Friday after work, and
we'd neck gin and scoff Scampi Fries and he'd have me
head spinnin' – Oh, he was a dirty divil – he'd have me
howlin' with the filth he'd been up to in the parks and
toilets of Birmingham.

KATARINA: What d'ya mean?

ELLEN: Don't worry about it.

But, er, when he didn't stop in one Friday, I thought
nothin' of it.

And when he didn't show up the next one, I thought, *fuck
ye George. Friday is me night.*

But I met this Kathy one, who said, did you hear what
happened Black George?

KATARINA: What happened 'im?

ELLEN: I'm gettin' there.

Beat.

He was attacked, wasn't he?

RACHEL: Oh no.

ELLEN: They got him somethin' awful. Collared by a group of
blokes in the park. Up on Cannon Hill?

RACHEL: Cannon Hill, yes.

ELLEN: Kicked the living shite out of him. He'd be up that way cruisin'.

KATARINA: Up what?

ELLEN: Don't ask.

Long as I live, I will never forget the shock and the fright that I got, when I walked through that door.

Oh, they savaged him.

They had him ruined, the bastards.

I barely recognised him.

They'd broken his bones – kicked him 'til his skull gave way – I mean – his eye sockets were fractured.

KATARINA: Dirty bastards.

ELLEN: Some man out walking his dog had found him, unconscious.

He'd been in a coma since.

I sat – jokin' with him and chattin' with him – hopin' he could hear me.

But I was terrified – I was sick leavin' that hospital.

Then when I got home I put the child to bed and I filled a cup of whiskey. One for me and a cup for Sean, and I says to Sean – *fuck me.*

The tears came as he grabbed me – to correct me language. The whiskey scorching me throat. The heart thumping in me chest. His long arm choking me as he held me in the middle of our living room.

We don't know we're alive, do we? We don't know we're alive.

And then he fucked me. As the young'un slept downstairs, he fucked me for the first and last time. The rest you would call duty. But he was boiling with passion that night.

And me thinking of George.

It was morning when the boy called in to work. I was
filling the salt shakers 'cos we did a toasted sandwich from
eleven. Reminded me of a neighbour of ours from home
what went off to be a priest./

WILL: *Ha ah ah ah*
Ha ah ah ah
Ha ah ah ah
Ha ah ah ah
Ha ah ah ah
Ha ah ah ah

ELLEN: /Pale white skin. Beautiful youngfella.

George is dead, he said.

And the dropped salt danced across the floor. The smashed
glass splashing from the tiles.

Begging the boy to stay then. Reaching out to him.
Clawing at him, hoping to find George in his – in his words
or in his touch. But he had his list to get through. Written
in George's address book – the names of the people he'd
cared 'bout.

My name, written down.

ALL: *Ooh ooh ooh ooh*
Ooh ooh ooh ooh
Ooh ooh ooh ooh
Ooh ooh ooh ooh
Ooh ooh ooh ooh
Ooh ooh ooh ooh
Ooh ooh ooh ooh
Ooh ooh ooh ooh

ELLEN: I stood in the rain round Snow Hill for what felt like
forever. Hoping the drains would drown me or swallow me
up. Hoping to God that I might just disappear.

Oh my God he was gorgeous, my gorgeous George.

Sean was shoutin' for his dinner when I walked in the door…

…And the words just came out.

I'm going home.

Beat.

You're not to come with me.

RACHEL: Just like that?

ELLEN: Followed by the roaring and crying and scratching and screaming. But yeah, just like that.

With William under me arm, and a suitcase full of fuck all, I crossed the Irish Sea.

RACHEL: You took his child away.

ELLEN: Sean never had time for William. He didn't go on the way fellas do with kids. Didn't take him to the football or joke around with him.

RACHEL: What about William though?

ELLEN: I made a choice.

Beat.

I thought we were comin' home – but it was all changed. Everyone was moved.

I cried 'til there was little left of me. Every day.

And Will – he was lost.

When we got a chance of this place we hopped on it. Our own flat. It was a start.

Fourteen, he would have been when we moved in here.

Willah he was christened on Dominick Street. Up and down the town.

My little English boy hangin' on street corners while I sat in the dark, cryin' and drinkin'. Not being a mother. Barely being anything. A stranger in this place, I was born. Too scared to step outside the door, to even go to the shops.

RACHEL: Dad's drinking made me never want to touch the stuff.

ELLEN: *(Raising a glass.)* Cheers.

RACHEL: I tasted champagne for the first time at my wedding.

KATARINA/ELLEN: Champagne!

RACHEL: It was my wedding.

Referencing the whiskey in her hand.

I don't drink.

Made a promise to myself not to wind up like he did. Sitting in that chair, shouting for a beer. *Rachel, get me a beer.* Comin' in from work, sittin' in that chair. Microwave dinner. Beer. Never going nowhere.

ELLEN: Well.

RACHEL: And it would soften him. I hated that the most. The drink would unlock something in him. He'd get all glassy eyed, lookin' at me:

You're all I've got.
You're everything.
You're all I've got.
The start and the end.

I didn't want to be all he had. I wanted a family.

Came time to go to Uni and I got as far away as possible. I got accepted to Edinburgh, and I was gone.

Summer holidays, I'd stay in Edinburgh. Doing nothing of value – just not going home.

And I thought, *of course I'll go home*, at some point, you know? But I met my Brian in my last year and then I found out I was pregnant, and I decided not to tell my Dad.

I'd kind of stopped calling by then. I'd stopped checking in.

We got engaged, me and Brian, but I wouldn't get married 'cos I didn't want to get married without my Dad there, and I didn't want my Dad there.

Daisy was two, we threw a party – just the neighbours and that – I think we had a bouncy castle – and people were getting upset because of an old drunk at our crossroads was asking 'bout me and about Daisy. My mate Stacey wanted the police called – but I wouldn't have it, because I knew I suppose.

Went up to the corner, and there he was.

In Edinburgh.

Drunk, but in Edinburgh.

His first ever train journey. And he'd liked it – because there was a bar.

I hadn't seen him in about four years.

He was the same old Dad. No better and no worse, but out of his chair and away from home he just looked like any sad old drunk.

A neighbour from home had seen me pushing a pram up the Royal Mile and grassed me up.

He didn't want anything. Didn't even want to come in. He just came to see we were okay. That Daisy was okay. He just wanted to know we were okay.

Then he panicked and pushed fifty pound into my hand and went off again.

You're all I've got.
You're everything.
You're all I've got.
The start and the end.

ELLEN: *You're all I've got.*
You're everything.
You're all I've got.
The start and the end.

BOTH: *You're all I've got.*
You're everything.
You're all I've got.

The start and the end.

WILL *hums one round of the melody.*

Pause.

ELLEN: Will would come home from school. His copy torn, or his knees scuffed – pushed around for his English accent, or whatever else they could pick at.

Fifteen. Black eyes.

Sixteen. Broken arm.

Seventeen. Smashed teeth.

There was a change in him then. A hardness to him.

Then word from his father to say that he wanted a divorce.

RACHEL: Dad?

ELLEN: 1987. The stupid fuck. You couldn't even buy a *johnny* in this town in 1987.

KATARINA: Ew. Is that true?

RACHEL: Was he going to marry my Mum?

ELLEN: Will went ballistic, punching at walls. *He was no Father anyway* – I'd be screamin'.

WILL: And what were you then?

ELLEN *looks to WILL.*

ELLEN: You don't count the cost of the sacrifices you make for your kids. You don't weigh the loss of the things that might have been. And you don't look for praise nor thanks, not anything. You just hope that they make it okay. That they are kind and happy and okay.

The knocking on the door started then. Look what your Willah has done. Smacked faces, robbed purses. My little English boy, the thug.

When he started to rob from me it was fecky things at first.

WILL: *(In harmony.)*

It was fecky things at first.

ELLEN: An ornament, an ashtray. Stupid things that you'd get nothing for.

WILL: **(In harmony.)** *Stupid things that you'd get nothing for.*

ELLEN: And then a fiver here and there.

WILL: **(In harmony.)** *And then a fiver here and there.*

ELLEN: I'd said nothing because, what's mine is his, and I just didn't want it to be true.

But I borrowed a thousand pound from a local fella who charges twenty-five per cent interest and gets very upset if you don't pay it back. It was to take us to Spain – our first holiday. Will had it took while I was in the bath. Before I'd even had it out of the envelope.

He was eighteen.

He better not walk across that door. The kind of thing you say to yourself until they don't walk across the door. Two weeks. Three.

And when he did, he was a different man. The gaunt face of his father staring at me.

From then on we was in this vile tug of war, cat and mouse, mother and addict. The house stripped of everything of value. The cutlery. The pots. I mean, the coal from the bunker. If he could get anything for it, it was gone.

It was a plague. Heroin was devouring the kids.

I used to batter him. I tried locking him in the house. Hiding his shoes. Anything to stop him walking out that door. And he'd fight me back, spitting and screaming, scratching and shouting. *If my Da was here*, he'd say.

WILL: **(In harmony.)** *If my Da was here.*

ELLEN: And I'd let him go, because I didn't have an answer for him.

KATARINA: You never told me none of this.

ELLEN: Ah, you don't be listenin' to me anyway. And what would be the value in tellin' it, other than looking for pity.

Beat.

I'm telling *her*…I'm telling you because…

RACHEL: He's my brother.

ELLEN: *(Firmly.)* No. Stop that now.

I'm telling you for Sean.

     Beat.

RACHEL: What happened to William?

    ELLEN shakes her head. She takes a deep breath.

Tell me.

     Long pause.

ELLEN: William had AIDS.

I've never said that out loud before.

Pneumonia. Complications from AIDS.

But *we* didn't call it that.

We buried that detail.

That's the way we do things here. We hide them.

It was 1993.

I hadn't seen Will since Christmas Eve. It was February and there was snow on the ground. I was burning newspapers for a bit of heat. Old shoes. Whatever would catch fire.

When he walked through the door that day…I…

Would you know what I meant if I said I could see him for the first time in years. My little English boy. My heart recognised him.

WILL: I'm sick Ma.

47

ELLEN: It was 'cos he needed me. But for that moment my heart heaved, 'cos I thought, he's back to me. He's come back to me.

I held him by the fire. Held him underneath my arms. Hugged him for forever. I thought, my little boy's come home.

WILL: I'm sick Ma.

ELLEN: But he was in a desperate way. His body burning. Oh God help him.

Too scared to see a doctor. Knew just what the sickness meant.

WILL: I was never far away Ma.

I was never far away.

I was never far away Ma.
I was never far away.

Ooh Ooh
Ooh Ooh
Ooh Ooh Ooh Ooh
Ooh Ooh Ooh Ooh
Ooh Ooh
Ooh Ooh
Ooh Ooh
Ooh Ooh Ooh
Ooh Ooh Ooh

I was never far away Ma.
I was never far away.

I was never far away Ma.
I was never far away.

ELLEN: *Would you know what I meant if I said, I could see him for the first time in years. My little English boy. Me heart recognised him.*

I buried him in a suit.

WILL: A tracksuit.

ELLEN: A tracksuit.

Beat.

That was his joke.

The women are silent. Pause.

I wrote to his father, but heard nothing back.

KATARINA: Like AIDS AIDS? Like gay AIDS?

ELLEN: If you had any brains you'd be dangerous.

Changing tone, to KATARINA.

It was carnage love. The kids were dropping like flies.

RACHEL: Dad didn't know.

ELLEN: I don't know.

RACHEL: He didn't.

ELLEN: I was very angry. And ashamed. I've carried that with me for a long time.

Pause.

RACHEL: What was he like, William?

WILL: *Gorgeous*, tell 'er.

ELLEN: He was a scumbag. He made life very difficult.

WILL: Give it a rest now.

ELLEN: But I adored him.

A door slams beneath the apartment.

BOBBY: *(From off stage.)* Kat? You in babe?

KATARINA's face lights up. She is in love.

KATARINA: Will I tell him I'll be up later?

ELLEN: Don't be silly now.

BOBBY: *(Offstage.)* Kit-Kat?

KATARINA: *(Calling to BOBBY.)* Shut up. I'm comin'.

BOBBY: *(Offstage.)* Baby – wait an' see you see what I'm after bringing home for you.

KATARINA: *(Beaming.)* He needn't think I'm waiting on him hand and foot now.

ELLEN: Get out you. You make me sick when you get all goo-goo ga-ga.

KATARINA: *(To RACHEL.)* You're all right you are.

> *KATARINA surprises RACHEL with a hug. KATARINA exits. The women stand awkwardly.*

ELLEN: I'm sorry now.

RACHEL: No.

ELLEN: You came all this way.

RACHEL: I'll go back now.

> *Pause.*

ELLEN: He *was* a good man – your Da. When he was eighteen, he pursued me like I was a rare and golden thing. He just had to have me. And we'd trip around Dublin glued to each other. The Adelphi Cinema or The Botanical Gardens. Anywhere it could just be the two of us.

> *Beat.*

I had almost forgotten about that.

> *Pause.*

I can see him in you now. Sean.

> *RACHEL closes her eyes. She might cry.*

RACHEL: Should I have brought my Dad back, do you think?

ELLEN: To this kip of a town?

RACHEL: I cremated him, see. The ashes are in the shed in our garden. My husband won't have them in the house. I'm thinking now I should have brought him here.

ELLEN: The dead don't care a dot. Use him as cement mixer.
It's all the one.

RACHEL looks at ELLEN for reassurance maybe.

Go home.

I mean home home.

Go home to your family.

*RACHEL reaches into her bag. She takes out a thick
envelope.*

RACHEL: Dad wanted William to have this.

Long pause.

It's money. He didn't have a lot, he didn't own the house
or anything, but he asked me to bring this to Dublin.

RACHEL puts it on the table.

ELLEN: I don't want it.

RACHEL: Dad said to me – just before he died – that he never
really knew how to be happy. He said Ireland taught him
about survival, but not happiness.

ELLEN: Yeah.

RACHEL: But he said, erm, he hoped you were happy. Yeah.
He just hoped you were.

Beat.

ELLEN: I just about survived.

Beat.

RACHEL: Is there something of William's I can have?

ELLEN: No.

RACHEL: Anything.

*ELLEN is frozen. She doesn't want to give anything
away.*

WILL: It's all just going in that attic anyway.

RACHEL: Please.

> *ELLEN fishes in a box. She produces a bear.*

ELLEN: Your Da got it in a jumble sale I think. Filthy aul' thing, but there was no talking to William. He loved it.

> *ELLEN hands the bear to RACHEL. RACHEL makes to exit.*

RACHEL: Will *is* my brother.

ELLEN: It's all past tense anyway.

RACHEL: He *is*.

ELLEN: Whatever you're looking for, I don't have it.

> *Beat.*

RACHEL: I was a bitch to my Dad.

ELLEN: I got that.

RACHEL: I wasn't ever there for him.

ELLEN: It's only guilt that'd make Sean sound so fucking amiable.

> *RACHEL laughs. She's upset.*

You loved him though.

Which means he was loved.

Which is enough.

> *Beat.*

You're okay.

> *ELLEN closes the door behind RACHEL. She is left alone with WILLIAM.*

You're lookin' at me now.

WILL: Am I?

> *ELLEN moves to the table. She takes the envelope. She considers opening it, then tosses it in the bin.*

ELLEN: It's all past tense.

KATARINA bursts through the door as ELLEN drinks.

KATARINA: What ya sayin'?

ELLEN: *(Annoyed.)* I'm saying you never get a minutes fuckin' peace around here.

KATARINA: Just sayin' to Bobby there, I think I'm gonna call me Ma.

ELLEN: *(Hopeful.)* Are you?

KATARINA: God, no. Fuck 'er. I'm gonna call *you* instead. I'm gonna call you every single day until you die. How about that?

ELLEN: You will not.

KATARINA: I fuckin' will an' all. Tormented you'll be. I'll have shares in that phone company by the time I'm finished with ya.

ELLEN: Get up them stairs you.

KATARINA: I'm gonna cook Bobby his dinner. He's after bringing in a load of tins. I'm cooking chickpea stew. I saw them making it on *This Morning*, this morning.

ELLEN: Stewed in what?

KATARINA: Curry sauce. It's all I've got.

KATARINA goes to exits. ELLEN stops her.

ELLEN: Kat.

ELLEN reaches into the bin. She pulls out the envelope.

Take this.

KATARINA: That's out of the bin you scumbag.

ELLEN: You take this, and you hide it. Listen to me now. You don't tell Bobby have it. You don't tell anyone. You keep that safe. D'ya hear me?

KATARINA: You're freakin' me out.

ELLEN: You're gonna do somethin' good with your life. You know that?

KATARINA: *(Surprised.)* Am I?

ELLEN: You fuckin' better.

Hide that now, until I'm gone and the child is popped out. You do what you like then.

KATARINA: You're scarin' me.

ELLEN: *(Joking.)* Boo.

KATARINA: *(Confused.)* What?

ELLEN: Just promise me.

KATARINA: Yeah, go on, I promise.

> **KATARINA snatches the envelope from ELLEN's hand.**

You are bananas missus.

> **KATARINA exits. ELLEN recoils into the room. Pause.**

ELLEN: I'm finished.

WILL: Cop on, will ya?

ELLEN: I'm done.

> **Beat.**

I've had enough.

WILL: Ma.

> **Pause.**

ELLEN: I walk out that door and I don't recognise any of it.

WILL: Don't be gammin' on Ma.

ELLEN: I don't recognise *meself* in any of it.

This used to be our town. Me and your Da.

We were so excited about leaving but.

England.

Everything would be great in England.

All the auld ones stood out in rows along the paths, banging pots as we lugged our cases up the road. It was some send off.

Banging their pots and singing, *Good Night, Good Night, Good Night & Good Luck.*

What happened us?

> *WILL's voice becomes faint.*

WILL: Stop.

ELLEN: What son?

WILL: You're a fighter Ma.

ELLEN: I can barely hear ya.

WILL: World champion, you are.

> *WILL disappears.*

ELLEN: The fight wears off but. It leaves you. I walk the streets of Dublin and I don't recognise them. I don't know them as me own. And worse. I'm invisible. I'm like a ghost walking around. People don't see me. They don't look at me. I'm just taking up space. I spent me life fighting to end up taking up space. That's this place, it is. That's us.

Will?

William?

> *ELLEN is left on the couch, surrounded by emptied boxes. The contents of her life around her.*

Come back to me son.
Come back and sit with me.

PHILLIP MCMAHON / RAYMOND SCANNELL

I was never far away.

FINISH